# What Your Colleagues Are Saying . . .

"Pariser and DeRoche draw from their own classroom experiences to provide a practical time management resource for classroom teachers. With thought-provoking questions at the end of each chapter, this text is a great springboard for collaborative conversations. *Real Talk About Time Management* is a resource I look forward to sharing and utilizing with the teachers in our system!"

**Julie Cantillon**
Associate Director, Office for Schools
Catholic Diocese of San Diego
San Diego, CA

"As a middle and high school English teacher, I often felt like there wasn't enough time in the day to get everything done. This struggle against the clock is one of the practical challenges I try to help the preservice teachers I now work with to prepare for, but considering time management frustrates even seasoned teachers, *Real Talk About Time Management* is a helpful tool. With assistance from sources as varied as Marie Kondo and YouTube car commercials, Serena and Ed provide accessible and applicable strategies for time management as well as tools for self-reflection and planning. Along with honest reflections and anecdotes, this book includes advice from actual teachers and realistic consideration of how preparation allows for successful teaching. Serena and Ed's applications are presented alongside a sense of respect for the significant workload and varied demands on teachers' time, which they also use to provide specific advice for tasks like grading, communication, and considering our workspaces. Two specific pieces of advice I appreciated from the authors were filtering the advice from others to best fit our needs and personalities and distinguishing between being busy and being productive. Ultimately, *Real Talk About Time Management* will help teachers to reprioritize their tasks and priorities and to optimize their work flow."

**Jason J. Griffith**
Assistant Professor of Education, Penn State University
State College, PA

"*Real Talk About Time Management* is exactly what busy teachers need! Even after nearly two decades of teaching, I found so many tips and strategies to streamline all the busyness of planning, grading, collaborating, interacting with parents, engaging students, and even the layout of the classroom. Ideas for dealing with mountains of paper as well as making sure to connect with colleagues are interspersed with heartwarming and hilarious stories of Ed's and Serena's classroom experiences. What a joy to read!"

**Janel Meehan**
English Language Arts Teacher, Grades 6 and 7
San Diego Unified School District
San Diego, CA

"*Real Talk About Time Management* is written in a comforting, practical style complemented with many thought-provoking, meaningful anecdotes and quotes. Offers excellent reminders and tips for K–12 teachers of any subject desiring to better manage their time in order to be more effective, more efficient, and more healthy caretakers. Deftly differentiates being busy from being productive and from tasks being important versus being urgent, and will help the dedicated teacher balance what they can control from what they cannot. The authors offer pragmatic resources, sharing perspectives from both a classroom teacher and a school administrator's lens. This book is a wonderful reference that will help educators work smarter, not harder. No-nonsense, applicable, and full of great tools and strategies for helping teachers better manage their time so that they can be their best in and out of the classroom."

**Harlan Klein**
Head of Middle School
The Bishop's School
La Jolla, CA

"An organized, thorough, and insightful book that captures real-life situations and strategies. A great read for any educator and administrator looking to make an immediate difference in the lives of children. A perfect read on strategies for establishing a work–life balance."

**Jennifer Shemtob**
Owner and CEO of Teacher Time to Go
Conshohocken, PA

"Serena Pariser gets right into the guts of our perennial problem: we don't have enough time! I can't imagine a more comprehensive or helpful book on time management for teachers. I hope it gets a wide and earnest reading."

**Dave Stuart Jr.**
Author, *These 6 Things*
Cedar Springs, Michigan

"The daily demands of elementary teachers such as responding to student and parent needs, curriculum preparation, academic reflection, collaboration with colleagues and administrative requirements can seem daunting. How necessary, important and valuable to have *Real Talk About Time Management,* a resource full of tools and practices to help balance the personal and professional lives of teachers!"

**Suzanne Hagan**
Elementary teacher
San Diego, CA

"Great read for someone just beginning their career and those that have been in the profession for years! I've been teaching for 22 years and learned so many new time management strategies that I am excited to implement in my classroom. I love how it uses real experiences and real life classroom situations making it relevant to teaching today. Thought provoking. Really gets you to reflect on yourself and how this translates into your teaching style. The strategies in this book can be applied not only in the classroom but also in everyday life."

**Michael Clarke**
Elementary teacher
Trappe, PA

# Real Talk About Time Management

*Most of us end up with no more than five or six people
who remember us. Teachers have thousands of people who remember
them for the rest of their lives. —Andy Rooney*

# Real Talk About Time Management

## 35 Best Practices for Educators

Serena Pariser and Edward F. DeRoche

FOR INFORMATION:

Corwin

A SAGE Company

2455 Teller Road

Thousand Oaks, California 91320

(800) 233-9936

www.corwin.com

SAGE Publications Ltd.

1 Oliver's Yard

55 City Road

London EC1Y 1SP

United Kingdom

SAGE Publications India Pvt. Ltd.

B 1/I 1 Mohan Cooperative Industrial Area

Mathura Road, New Delhi 110 044

India

SAGE Publications Asia-Pacific Pte. Ltd.

18 Cross Street #10-10/11/12

China Square Central

Singapore 048423

Acquisitions Editor:  Ariel Curry

Development Editor:  Desirée A. Bartlett

Associate Content

    Development Editor:  Jessica Vidal

Editorial Intern:  Nyle DeLeon

Production Editor:  Tori Mirsadjadi

Copy Editor:  Shannon Kelly

Typesetter:  C&M Digitals (P) Ltd.

Proofreader:  Rae-Ann Goodwin

Indexer:  Robie Grant

Cover and Interior Designer:  Scott Van Atta

Marketing Manager:  Margaret O'Connor

Printed in Canada

*Library of Congress Cataloging-in-Publication Data*

Names: Pariser, Serena, author. | DeRoche, Edward F., author.

Title: Real talk about time management: 35 best practices for educators / Serena Pariser, University of San

Diego, USA, Edward F. DeRoche, University of San Diego, USA.

Description: Thousand Oaks, California : Corwin, [2020] | Series: Corwin teaching essentials; Volume 1 | Includes bibliographical references and index.

Identifiers: LCCN 2019042287 | ISBN 9781544376912 (paperback) | ISBN 9781544376929 (epub) | ISBN 9781544376936 (epub) | ISBN 9781544376905 (pdf)

Subjects: LCSH: Teachers—Job stress—Prevention. | Time management. | Burn out (Psychology)—Prevention.

Classification: LCC LB2840.2 .P37 2020 | DDC 158.7/2—dc23

LC record available at https://lccn.loc.gov/2019042287

This book is printed on acid-free paper.

20 21 22 23 24 10 9 8 7 6 5 4 3 2 1

# Contents

Note From the Publisher: The authors have provided video and web content throughout the book that is available to you through QR (quick response) codes. To read a QR code, you must have a smartphone or tablet with a camera. We recommend that you download a QR code reader app that is made specifically for your phone or tablet brand.

# Acknowledgments

Corwin gratefully acknowledges the contributions of the following reviewers:

Meghan Love
K–5 ESOL teacher
Springfield Elementary
Fort Mill, SC

Lyneille Meza
Director of data & assessment
Denton ISD
Denton, TX

Amanda McKee
High school algebra instructor
Johnsonville High School
Johnsonville, SC

Elisa Waingort
Grade 5 teacher
W.O. Mitchell School
Calgary, Alberta, Canada

# About the Authors

**Serena Pariser, MA,** has twelve years of experience teaching in public schools, including charter schools from kindergarten through twelfth grade. She served as an eighth- and ninth-grade ELA teacher for nine years at Gompers Preparatory Academy. She has taught in some of the most challenging school settings from coast to coast, including a boarding school for students from fifteen different Indian tribes in South Dakota, North Dakota, and Nebraska. Most of her full-time teaching experience is at the middle school level, although she also has experience in high school and elementary school settings. She earned her bachelor's degree in education at Pennsylvania State University and her master's degree in educational technology from San Diego State University. She has been a teacher, teacher coach, and curriculum designer, and she has held leadership positions in K–12 school settings and university settings. Serena was humbled to be recognized as teacher of the year at Gompers Preparatory Academy in the 2008–2009 school year.

Serena presents at conferences state-wide and nationally on topics ranging from character education to classroom management. In June 2018 she was a keynote speaker at the Beginning Institute in Tucson, Arizona. For two years she served as the assistant director of field experience at the University of San Diego, where she had the opportunity to work closely with master's degree students entering the teaching profession. She continues to teach graduate courses on classroom management and character education.

In addition to her work in the United States, Serena has expanded her educational knowledge around the globe. She coached teachers and modeled best practices and engagement strategies in Kathmandu, Nepal, and also taught in rural parts of Turkey.

Serena was selected as a U.S. ambassador by the Fulbright Distinguished Teaching Program. Fulbright gave her an opportunity to coach eleventh- and twelfth-grade teachers in a rural village in Botswana on engagement strategies, smart technology use, and best practices in the classroom.

Serena is the bestselling author of *Real Talk About Classroom Management: 50 Best Practices That Work and Show You Believe in Your Students*, published by Corwin in February 2018. It has also been made into a self-paced online video course, Skillbuilders, for both new and experienced teachers. Serena relocated to Minneapolis, Minnesota, to be closer to her family.

Twitter: @SerenaPariser

Facebook: www.facebook.com/serenapariser

Blog: www.serenapariser.com

E-mail: serena.pariser@gmail.com

**Edward F. DeRoche, MA, MS, PhD**, has been an elementary and middle school teacher and principal, a public school board member, a member of two private high school boards, a professor, a program evaluator, a student adviser, a teacher trainer, and the University of San Diego's School of Education dean.

Ed was a past president of the California Association of Teacher Educators and a member of the National Commission on Character Education. Currently he is the director of the Character Education Resource Center in the School of Leadership and Education Sciences at the University of San Diego.

With Professor Mary M. Williams, he co-authored one of Corwin's first books on character education, titled *Educating Hearts and Minds: A Comprehensive Character Education Framework*, which is a concise and practical guide for practitioners.

Quality character education doesn't happen without quality leadership at the top. Ed filled a gap in the character education literature by writing *Character Education: A Guide for School Administrators*.

No field can flourish without methods of assessing effectiveness. Ed filled another gap with his book *Evaluating Character Development: 51 Tools for Measuring Success.*

Ed's eight books and more than fifty journal articles constitute an impressive record of scholarship, and he is also the author of the Character Education Resource Center's monthly newsletter, *New You Can Use*, as well as a monthly blog.

He is a consultant, evaluator, author, teacher trainer, and a recipient of several awards, including the Sanford N. McDonald Award for Lifetime Achievement in Character Education from Character.org, the University of San Diego's School of Education's Outstanding Administrator of the Year Award, and the *San Diego Union-Tribune's* Educator of the Year Award.

Under Ed's leadership, the School of Education offered educators the opportunity to earn a master's degree in character education, one of the first advanced degrees in the field. In addition, the Character Education Resource Center pioneered online teacher training in character education for both graduate and professional credit. Now in its twenty-fourth year, the center continues to offer its popular summer conference Character Matters.

Ed is honored to be the co-author of this time management book with Serena and appreciates her advice and counsel as a member of the Character Education Resource Center's Advisory Committee. Ed can be reached at character@sandiego.edu. Feel free to reach out to sign up for his monthly *News You Can Use* blog or just to e-mail.

[Ed] This book is dedicated to the many teachers in my life (they know who they are) who took the time to advise me, counsel me, guide me, befriend me, warn me, tolerate me, and contribute to my love of teaching and administering.

[Serena] This book is dedicated to my grandpop, who kept his life simple so he could always get everything done. May we all be so lucky.

# Introduction

· · · · · · · · · · · · · · · · · · · · · · · · · · · · · · · · · · · · · · · · · · ·

*Roughly 61 percent of educators said their work was "always" or "often" stressful, compared with American workers, in general, citing their work was stressful 30 percent of the time, according to a new survey released by the American Federation of Teachers.*

*—Joel Stice, writing for Education World*

Yet it's also reported that over 96 percent of teachers love their jobs. Let's face it, we love what we do, we just want to be able to feel less stressed each day doing it.

If we could give you more minutes in the day, how would you use your extra time? Did you know that there are 1,440 minutes in a day? It rarely ever feels that way, especially in our classrooms. Raise your hand if you've ever heard a teacher say that they're stressed or overwhelmed—or if you've ever said the same thing. If your hand is not up, you are either the luckiest teacher in the world or . . . well . . . *cough* lying.

To be honest, stress isn't all entirely negative. Actually, a little bit of stress can be helpful in motivating us to perform. We don't need time management skills when we are on a Caribbean vacation, but we do need them in the classroom. Why? Time management is important when you have a series of tasks to do. That's teaching. Our success in time management—before class, during instruction, after class, and even in our personal life—can have a real effect on our teaching, for better or worse. It all comes back to the classroom. Time management doesn't mean that you'll never feel stressed again, but hopefully the tools in this book will help you mitigate stress on a daily basis.

As stated in the quote above, just under half of us feel stressed daily (46 percent). Ed and I have found ways to keep ourselves with the 54 percent of educators who have found positive means to handle stressful situations. We'd like to share with you what has worked for us.

[Serena] When Ed offered to join me for this book I quickly agreed. Why? Ask anybody who knows him and they will tell you he is one of the best time managers you will ever meet. I mean that. I have yet to meet anybody who can

*(Continued)*

(Continued)

manage time like Ed. He makes it seem so easy, always has a smile on his face, and gets things done quickly and thoroughly. He's accomplished more in his lifetime than most and still always seems to have time for friends and family and to lend a helping hand. Also, Ed gives the time management perspective from his many years in not only teaching but also in administrating both an elementary and a middle school, and I bring in the perspective of a teacher. You'll find both perspectives to be equally valuable.

Like Ed, I'm exceptionally skilled at time management. Together we will share what works. Some of these best practices we've discovered on our own, and some we have borrowed from others over the years. We're going to tell it to you like it really is: Time management directly relates to classroom management, your personal sanity, and your overall quality of life inside and outside of the classroom. It's all about how we manage our workload, manage our time, and have a healthy mindset about our responsibilities. We have two personal stories to share.

[Serena] I've been there. It was December, right before winter break to be exact, during my first year as a classroom teacher. I was a sixth-grade teacher at a charter school in West Philadelphia. A few months in, I had made up my mind: I was done. I would put in my resignation midyear. I felt stuck. The tasks had piled up too high, I didn't feel like I was getting anywhere with my twenty-nine rambunctious sixth graders, and I had too many angry parents. The only way out was to quit. I would cut my losses and walk.

In an effort to try to get some moral support, I knocked on the door of my neighboring teacher, Mr. Davis. He had been my lifeline so far that year. As I described my feelings of failure and being completely overwhelmed, he simply said, "You can't leave your first year teaching. You'll get through it." I scraped my pride off of the floor and took his advice. I stayed and completed the first year of what later turned out to be the profession of my dreams.

What changed?

For starters, I stopped working in my classroom late hours every evening. I learned to take breaks and balance myself, even if the work wasn't done. I asked for help when I knew there was an easier way to do something in the classroom. Neighboring teachers started sharing organizational tricks that saved me many precious minutes. These were just a few of the time management techniques that kept me in the classroom that year.

I realized that having strong time management skills was the most important factor in being able to manage stress on the job. It directly affected my ability to connect with students, actually smile while teaching, and have an enormous amount of job satisfaction. I gained control of my classroom, and I wasn't going home mentally exhausted anymore. More importantly, I didn't feel like a hamster on a wheel. I knew where to put my energy, how to work efficiently, how to produce the same if not better results in my classroom, how to have more energy to connect with students, and how to have fun while teaching. Many of the strategies I learned that year are covered in the chapters in this book.

Also, I brought Ed on board to add another perspective. Ed and I met at a conference at the University of San Diego, and he invited me to do a workshop with teachers after my eighth-grade classroom participated in his writing contest. I immediately noticed his remarkably strong time management skills, his dedication to keeping his work–life balance, and the amount he has accomplished with this mindset. He's also here to share his experience.

[Ed] Probably like you, time management is and has been a constant factor in my personal and professional life. One example from my years as a principal comes to mind.

Many of the new teachers I supervised (as well as a few veterans) had similar time management problems as Eileen, a first-year teacher for our sixth-grade students. We liked Eileen; we were influenced by her talents, attitude, and enthusiasm. However, Eileen "overplanned" everything and anything. Her supervising teacher and I had talked to her about this when she was a student teacher, noting that it was not healthy and could increase the stress level of being a teacher. Eileen would spend hours developing unit and lesson plans, often after school was over. Leaving at 5 p.m. was not unusual for her, and I frequently found myself saying, "Eileen, you cannot stay later than the principal— it's time to go home!" This behavior occurred at home as well. She was only one month into her full-time teaching position and I found her volunteering for any activity that was going on at the school. In her classroom, every minute of every day had been mapped out, in writing, noting what she and her students would be doing that day and that week.

In early October, Eileen came into my office showing "end of the day" exhaustion, near tears and frustrated. We began our discussion. After an hour, during which she did most of the talking, we set up another meeting. She shared her belief that if her students were not busy (working), they were

*(Continued)*

(Continued)

not learning. According to her, "If I don't keep them busy, I'm going to have discipline problems," and "What we can't get done in class we will get done at home (homework)."

What Eileen didn't know was that her student teacher supervisor had already alerted me to this situation. Eileen also didn't know that a couple of parents had inquired about the amount of homework their kids had to do. I asked Eileen if she wanted help, and she said yes. So, along with her student teacher supervisor and a few others, I worked with her throughout the year. Many of the strategies, techniques, and tips that you will find in this book were part of our work with Eileen. Note that by her fourth year at our school, Eileen had become one of the more popular student teacher supervisors.

We surveyed twenty-five of our K–12 teacher colleagues, asking what they considered to be the major time management problems or issues for teachers. While this certainly wasn't a scientific study, the results rang true with what we've seen in the research and in our own experience. In summary, here is what they told us, in no particular order:

- ▶ Grading student work

- ▶ Carving out co-planning time

- ▶ Planning units and lessons; finding resources

- ▶ Organizing classroom materials, displays, and/or supplies

- ▶ Scheduling and attending meetings; co-curricular activities and similar responsibilities

- ▶ Paperwork—staying on top of e-mails from teachers, administrators, and parents

- ▶ Developing and monitoring groupwork

- ▶ Balancing long-term goals of curriculum and assignments with the social, emotional, and academic goals of children

- ▶ Organizing the day—prioritizing the work that has to be done or the curriculum that has to be presented

- ▶ Finding time to meet with individual students

- ▶ Allowing for differentiation (e.g., extra time, modifications of a task, providing enrichment)

▶ Technology—much preparation and planning time is spent on e-mailing with parents, posting notices, etc.

▶ Finding time for enough writing instruction, practice, reflection, and sharing

▶ Practicing empathy—forcing yourself to consider the needs of others and your organization when deciding how to use any discretionary time

▶ Stop seeking balance and find the usage of time that makes you the best version of yourself; that means taking time to "recharge"

The teachers we interviewed also expressed frustration as they reported to us the following:

▶ "I have no time. When I arrive at school, I am trapped between the two covers of our textbook and the four walls of the classroom."

▶ "I'm trying to handle twelve- to fifteen-hour days. I have almost no time to do some of the things I should be doing—things that need to get done for the benefit of my students."

▶ "You really want to know how I see it—I am overworked, I have to attend unproductive meetings, and I am drowning in testing and paperwork."

We hear you. We've been there. We can help.

We address these topics as best practices in this book in a real and practical way. We'll show you strategies that you can start using on day one. We also include strategies that have worked for us time and time again. These practices helped us manage our time as we changed roles, moved classrooms, and so on. Learning these strategies took us both years of practice and lots of wasted time and frustration. We're here to save you a bit of both.

To add to our fun, we went back and asked the same twenty-five educators one other question: "If we could give you more minutes in the day, how would you spend your time?" One teacher said she wouldn't spend her time answering survey questions, and another replied, "How can you ask me this question when I'm trying to get my classroom ready for school?" The others were too inundated with preparing for a new school year to answer. We get it: You're busy. You're really, really busy.

Here's the bottom line: Teachers that are good time managers have students that are engaged and actively listening.

We all want that.

## About This Book

As you read and implement these strategies, we encourage you to be a risk-taker and a problem-solver. Take our advice, tweak it, modify it, and make it work for you.

We spent some time finding the cutting-edge research on time management strategies (that you might not have time to find yourself) and paired this research with our own experiences to provide suggestions for you and your classroom. Our intention isn't to regurgitate time management tips you've heard time and time again. Our intention is to give you the opportunity to take a step back and see where you can make a few small (or perhaps large) adjustments to make a significant difference in the amount of time you could be saving—or gaining. We'd like to make it seem like you actually have more minutes in the day.

In this book you will receive the following:

- ❱ Strategies that have worked over and over again to save time and energy in your classroom

- ❱ Research from the experts about time management and personal wellness

- ❱ Real stories about time management from teachers currently in the field

The real value of the book becomes apparent when you get up on the "balcony" and look down at your classroom, taking "snapshots" of the transformation that has happened and noting how the changes in your time management plan have worked.

Some of the most important things to realize about effective time management are that it will improve your confidence and morale, it will energize and engage your students (and their parents), and it will change the climate of your classroom. Most teachers will testify to one important truth: Good classroom and time management makes for a healthy learning environment for both you and the students.

—Serena and Ed

*Before we start this book, we ask that you take three deep breaths. It's important to stop, breathe, and slow down to speed up.*

*And remember, always make time for relationships, personal growth, and family.*

*—Serena and Ed*

# PART I

## TIME MANAGEMENT MINDSET

There is one way to achieve time management. And that is . . . to get it done. Time management is a tricky thing. We all have our own way, our own system. Something that works for one person may not work for another.

The most powerful advice I have ever received was learned through showing, not telling. According to Jennifer, a second grade teacher in Pennsylvania,

> My parents are two of the most incredibly driven and motivated people I know. Both lawyers but with extremely different styles. I can vividly remember visiting them at their office. I walked into my mom's office and there were papers flying everywhere. Aggressive typing, yellow notepads with scribbles, and phone calls occurring. Next, I walked across the hall to my father's office. One pad of paper on his desk. A single blue pen perfectly aligned to his pad of paper. And my father, completing a task and checking it off.
>
> They worked in the same law office and are both extremely successful lawyers . . . how could one place have two totally different styles? It's taken me quite some time to come to the realization . . . but case in point . . . find what works for you, become good at "your way" and make it happen.

# Ask Yourself Questions

*If I had an hour to solve a problem and my life depended on the solution, I would spend the first fifty-five minutes determining the proper question to ask, for once I know the proper question, I could solve the problem in less than five minutes.*

*—Albert Einstein*

As teachers, we are persistent question askers. We ask questions every day in our classroom when we are checking on our students' behaviors and seeking to discover what they are learning. Questions guide us to understand what our students know and comprehend and help us decide where we need to go from there. They help us unpack what is going on inside the students' minds.

Let's apply this art of asking questions to ourselves and take a reflective look at how we are spending our time and what we might need to adjust to be able to do the things we want to do. Think of time as a limited resource, similar to money. You plan now to have more for later.

Ask yourself these questions:

- *How* am I spending my time?
- *What* tasks should I be doing and why? What do I want to accomplish this week/this prep/this hour?
- *Why* is this important?
- *When* is the best time to do these tasks?
- *Where* is the best place to do these tasks?

We'll address the answers to these questions in the chapters to come.

Let's take a look at how you are doing with time. Circle the number that corresponds with how you feel right now for each statement.

| | STRONGLY AGREE | AGREE | SOMETIMES AGREE | DISAGREE |
|---|---|---|---|---|
| On a day-to-day basis, I get everything done that I need to get done. | 4 | 3 | 2 | 1 |
| I feel in control of my task list at work and at home. | 4 | 3 | 2 | 1 |
| I spend as much time with friends and loved ones as I'd like. | 4 | 3 | 2 | 1 |
| I have time to pursue personal interests outside of work. | 4 | 3 | 2 | 1 |
| I feel like I have time to connect with students and colleagues daily. | 4 | 3 | 2 | 1 |

_____ **Average (Mean) Score**

**Score:**

16–20: If you have a mean score of 16–20, you're doing well with time management. You probably feel like you have a healthy work–life balance, but you might be looking for strategies to up your game even more.

12–15: After a few years in the classroom, most of us are probably in this range. Most of the time you feel like you have your time management under control, but you'd like to have more control consistently throughout the entire year.

8–11: We're here to help! You're thirsty for time management strategies that could greatly improve your classroom, your mental health, and your life. We got you.

7 or below: Let's take this one step at a time. We've all been there.

Take a few minutes to reflect on your score. Use the questions below to guide your thinking or share with a friend or colleague. Taking some time to reflect and ask questions can reveal to ourselves the decisions we are subconsciously making day to day regarding how we spend our time.

## Your Turn

1. What was your average score? What would you like it to be?

2. What do you think is the cause of the discrepancy, if there is one?

3. Where did you develop the time management skills you use today?

STRATEGY #2

# Be Tuned in to the Advice Other Teachers Give You About Time Management

*Nobody has made it through life without somebody else's help.*

> —Heather French Henry, veterans advocate,
> fashion designer, and former Miss America

Some teachers make teaching seem easy. They float around their classrooms with a smile on their face, making gentle, quick, and genuine connections with students as they deliver their lessons with grace and wit. The students are on the edge of their seats eagerly awaiting the teacher's next words.

Let us pause for a second. It's so important to understand how much preparation goes on behind the scenes for this to happen. This teacher most likely had years of figuring out how to grade piles of paper and still get enough sleep to be present to teach the next day. This type of teacher most likely has really effective time management skills. The point is that all teachers have their own personal time management strategies, but there are a few strategies that usually work most, if not all, of the time. You'll find many of those strategies in this book. When speaking to other teachers, listen to the advice they give you and give it your own personal twist. If it doesn't work, try something else because eventually something will work really well for you.

[Serena] One of my very first professional developments as a year-one teacher occurred the first time I realized that some advice will work for you in the classroom and some will not. I was teaching thirty-eight sixth graders in an inner-city charter school in West Philadelphia. They were often unengaged, yelling at each other and at me. I did everything I could to get them to stay in their seats. I considered myself more of a circus ringmaster than a teacher. Furthermore, even though my credential was in English, I was teaching mathematics. It was a recipe for disaster. On top of my classroom management being *cough* subpar, my time management skills were lacking dramatically. I found myself often focusing on the wrong things in the classroom. My health was deteriorating. I felt tired, chugging coffee all day just to be able to make it to dismissal. Piles of papers were growing by the minute on my desk. I usually planned the following day's lesson around 7 p.m. the night before, after I had had a second to eat a warm meal after each hectic day. I was a hamster on a wheel.

My principal had invited in a veteran teacher from another school, Ms. Lilac, to provide professional development. I remember her flowy bright colors, large earrings, and the vibrant personality of her hair. Students loved her warm smile, graceful way of talking, and the way she half closed her bright eyes when she sang her next words. She spoke about the importance of connecting with children as you are teaching. *Yes!* I thought. *This is what I have been missing. I need to connect to my sixth graders.*

Ms. Lilac talked about the importance of gentle touch. She walked up and down the rows of teachers, gently touching each one of us on the shoulder as she delivered her message. I felt connected to her and her warmth. Her gentle touch was effective as it made me feel more connected to her and how she was teaching us to connect with the students in our classrooms.

The next day I started mimicking Ms. Lilac. As I robotically explained a long division problem, I walked up and down the rows and gently poked each child's shoulder with my cold finger. The reaction was the exact opposite of any sort of connection. There was a lot of "What the heck?!?" and confused looks, and one student even slid under his seat before I reached his desk to avoid my cold prod.

The point is that all teachers have advice for what works for them. Touch worked for Ms. Lilac but not for me. But she did teach me other useful strategies that helped me in my journey to becoming a better teacher.

[Ed] Like Serena, I had my Ms. Lilac. In fact, I had two. I was the "rookie" junior high teacher, teaching social studies and civics, and they were the veterans—Andy teaching mathematics and science; Alice teaching English/language arts. For three years, Andy and Alice gave me advice, suggestions, and, at times, counseling.

One day during my first year, the other teachers and I were getting our classrooms ready before school began the following week. Alice and Andy walked into my classroom, introduced themselves, and shared a little with me about the school, the kids, the parents, and the administration. I will never forget this. Alice said, "Ed, we are a team. The better you do, the better Andy and I do. After all, the three of us are teaching the same kids and dealing with the same parents. We are here to help you be a good, successful teacher."

I kept a notebook of their recommendations. Their advice carried me through years of successful teaching and administrative duties. Their recommendations included the following:

- Use to-do lists

- Plan. Plan. Plan for the month, the week, and the day; prioritize

- Don't grade everything

- Let students assist with class routines and tasks

During my career as an educator, I have tried to be an Alice and Andy to others. Their greatest contribution was in training and inspiring educators like me to be mentors to new generations of educators.

Pick and choose what works for you, but most importantly, listen to model teachers. Ask them what strategies they use for grading, for keeping their classroom clean, for dealing with tardy students, or even for managing student bathroom use during class. Perhaps these strategies can save you some time and energy. Let's all share our knowledge with others.

## Your Turn

1. Describe one time-saving technique you use in your classroom management, planning, or grading that works for you. Where did you learn this strategy?

2. What is one aspect of classroom management on which you would like some advice for how to save time?

STRATEGY
#3

# You Have So Much to Do—Why?

*When everything seems to be going against you, remember that the airplane takes off against the wind, not with it.*

—*Henry Ford*

We will be up front with you by giving you a direct answer to the question above. You have so much to do because you are a teacher. There will never be enough time. That's the nature of our profession. We have worked with teachers who handled their workload effectively, we've worked with teachers who got stressed daily, and we've sadly worked with teachers who "burned out" and started cutting corners (e.g., giving students worksheets so the teacher could take a break, taking sick days, leaving school at the sound of the bell).

According to the 2017 Educator Quality of Work Life Survey, which captured the data of nearly 5,000 teachers and staff, "Educators and school staff find their work 'always' or 'often stressful' 61 percent of the time, significantly higher than workers in the general population, who report that work is 'always' or 'often' stressful only 30 percent of the time" (Badass Teachers Association, 2017). In a short piece titled "Why Teachers Quit," Elizabeth Mulvahill quoted a teacher who succinctly described the stress teachers are under: "We get bombarded with paperwork, ridiculous curriculum, and lack of time along with unrealistic expectations" (Mulvahill, 2019).

But remember, 95 percent of you love your jobs. Hold on to that love.

So what can you do about all that you have to do? We have seven suggestions that work for us. We hope they work for you too.

1.  **Be prepared**. You are in a very busy profession: Admit it, deal with it, and prepare yourself for it. Prioritize what you plan to do each day based on what you can realistically accomplish.

2.  **Be in control**. This means take charge of what you and others want you to do and be realistic about your limits. Set manageable objectives and develop a plan to implement them. Don't be afraid to ask for feedback on how you are doing. Catch yourself when you get distracted and get back on track.

3.  **Be collaborative.** Teaching can be a lonely profession. Do not let it be so for you. Engage in meaningful exchanges with colleagues, administrators, parents, and educators in your community. Join education organizations. Teach a unit with your grade-level team. Collaborators can be a valuable resource for managing time, enriching instruction, and expanding your network of support. Two minds are often better than one. And three minds are often better than two . . . you get the idea.

4.  **Be positive**. You will experience ups and downs in this profession. Research suggests that positive emotions are contagious. Your students will remember some of what you say but a great deal of how you made them feel. Our advice: Celebrate all positive events in and out of school with people you care for.

5.  **Be purposeful.** You had a reason, a purpose for becoming a teacher. You had an interest in working with children and young people. Your purpose was captured in your commitments, your objectives, and your motivations to do what you love to do. Your teaching purpose is fueled by your desire to teach the young, to collaborate with others, to become a member of the team and maybe its leader. Your purpose is your sense of developing the "whyness" of things and finding out what works and what doesn't.

6.  **Be a problem-solver.** To solve a problem you have to know that you have one and what its complexities are. In general, we suggest this problem-solving framework:

    Step 1—Identify the problem.

    Step 2—Examine potential solutions.

    Step 3—Develop and implement one or more of the solutions.

Step 4—Assess whether or not your solutions solved the problem.

Step 5—Decide whether the problem is solved or if you should repeat steps 1–4.

7. **Know the difference between busy and productive.** We need to constantly ask ourselves: *Am I just staying busy or am I being productive?*

| BUSY | PRODUCTIVE |
|---|---|
| ✓ Stressed and/or anxious | ✓ Do tasks from start to finish |
| ✓ Reactive mode—rushing to do everything so nothing "explodes" | ✓ Start tasks with an optimal mindset |
| ✓ Putting out fires | ✓ You decide when you start the task |
| ✓ Went into task with a depleted mindset | ✓ A sense of accomplishment and happiness when task is accomplished |
| ✓ The task is started because it can't wait any longer | |
| ✓ A sense of relief when task is finished | |
| Examples: | Examples: |
| ▶ Not being prepared with lessons, leading to multiple behavior issues. Much time is now needed to call home to parents. | ▶ Scheduling a time to prepare materials for a lesson the week before you teach it |
| ▶ Answering numerous parent questions 1:1 | ▶ Sending out a semester newsletter so parents can stay up to date with your classroom |
| ▶ Answering numerous student questions about grades 1:1 | ▶ Setting aside time each week to complete grading and giving students grade reports every two weeks |

## Your Turn

1. In past month or so, would you say you were more busy or productive? Why is that and do you need to change something?

2. What part of your job do you absolutely love? As you start taking things off your plate, be sure not to discard your favorite activities.

3. How many of the seven tips are you already doing? Which of them work for you? Is there one you'd like to start doing in the future? Is there something we may have left out? Please share your ideas.

STRATEGY
#4

# Be a Hunter—Track Down Controllable Factors That Add to Your Workload

*If a doctor, lawyer, or dentist had forty people in his office at one time, all of whom had different needs, and some of whom didn't want to be there and were causing trouble, and the doctor, lawyer, or dentist, without assistance, had to treat them all with professional excellence for nine months, then he might have some conception of the classroom teacher's job.*

—*Donald D. Quinn*

[Ed] It is interesting that my conversations with Serena about strategies meant to help teachers in the classroom invariably take us outside the classroom.

We have different points of view about "workload"—Serena's comes from her years as a classroom teacher, and mine comes from my years as an administrator. Our discussions lead to one observation: Addressing matters

*(Continued)*

> (Continued)
>
> of workload in the classroom inevitably brings up workload issues outside the classroom.
>
> So, we look for a balance—focusing here on classroom workload and appreciating the fact that workload issues also occur in other contexts (home, community, church). One of my favorite pieces of advice about how to get control of our workload is to actually understand where to surrender control.

*Life is a balance between what we can control and what we cannot. I am learning to live between effort and surrender.*

—*Danielle Orner*

When we talk about workload here we are going to narrow it only to school work as best we can. We all know how difficult it can be for teachers to manage a teaching workload, committee work, and parent conferences, as well as also manage their workload outside of school.

Workload can vary dramatically depending on the grade level you teach, the number of students in your class(es), and your students' needs and interests. For the most part, elementary teachers teach all subjects to classrooms of approximately thirty students. Middle and high school teachers teach in a departmental format, perhaps teaching three to five subjects and 100 or more students each day.

Unfortunately, much of your workload is likely dictated by factors outside your control. Below are examples of factors that are in your control and factors that are often not in your control that could add to your workload.

| IN YOUR CONTROL | OFTEN NOT IN YOUR CONTROL |
|---|---|
| How you seat students so they can collaborate with one another | Class size |
| Systems in place for completing paperwork | Paperwork you receive |
| Systems you create for addressing/redirecting off-task behaviors | Off-task behaviors from students |
| How you use your limited time in prep periods | Number of prep periods |

| IN YOUR CONTROL | OFTEN NOT IN YOUR CONTROL |
| --- | --- |
| The amount of nonclassroom, before-school, and after-school activities you decide to commit to in addition to your teaching load | Amount of extracurricular activities in a school |
| Systems in place for how and when you grade | Amount of grading to be completed |

[Ed] For example, my first year in the classroom I taught a different class each period. I was "low man on the totem pole" and got the "leftovers"—which is often (but not always) the case for first-year teachers. This was a factor I could not control.

Researchers at Bradley University found that larger workloads for teachers adversely affected students' experience. According to these researchers, "If faculty are dissatisfied with their workload, feel overwhelmed, and find themselves not achieving good student results, they suffer, and consequently, students suffer" (James, 2015). So, when teachers are happy with their workload, it shows in the classroom and most importantly impacts student relationships.

We spoke with Jennifer Zimmermaker, an education specialist at Mesa Verde Middle School in Poway, California. She shared some advice that has helped her tremendously with her workload.

# WORK SMARTER, NOT HARDER

My mother-in-law's words still echo in my ears as she explained to me one of the most essential anecdotes to teacher burnout: "Work smarter, not harder." I remember that at the time I loved the meaning of the platitude but wasn't sure how to put it into practice. I was working through my lunch and prep with the hopes that I could come home early, only to find myself still having to use the flashlight on my phone to navigate the long hallway from my classroom to the parking lot where mine would be the only car under the dark evening sky. I would come home to find that my husband, who had prepared dinner based on my wishful thinking ETA, had already eaten and was ready for bed. I realized that I had to take my mother-in-law's words and mantra to heart and start embodying her advice for a more balanced work and home life by finding innovative strategies that would help me get more work done in less time.

Below are some techniques that changed my workday for the better and ensured that I was able to have more quality time for those I love, including myself:

- I started to use my prep more efficiently by creating a to-do list of the most important pending items—limiting this list to two to three items. This helped make me feel more productive, and I was able to shut off distractions and really get to work.

- I also would do the thing I dreaded the most first instead of putting it off for last. This also helped me because I was no longer procrastinating and just got it done so I could enjoy that feeling of accomplishment that I felt afterwards.

- I set a timer so I could try to be more consistent in the time I left school, keeping my promise to my husband. I started to leave at 4:30 p.m. every day knowing that there was no way to get everything completed but that the work would always be there and moments with family are more fleeting than that. This also allowed me to make sure I was able to have quality time to eat dinner with my husband.

- I made time for self-care by booking monthly massages, sometimes scheduling them at 3:45 p.m. to ensure that I left school immediately after the buses. I would also pack my gym clothes and bring them to school with me. Then I would change before I left to ensure that I went to the gym. This was such a nice change from my old habit of coming home with the intentions of going to the gym but never leaving my house because I was just too exhausted.

- I stopped checking my work e-mail or bringing work home on the weekends, knowing that the time I spent at school would be more productive. When I took the time to really heed my mother-in-law's advice, my smarter and more time-efficient habits helped me not only be a more successful teacher but a more balanced and content human being who was nurturing my relationships with loved ones.

In 2003 Robert Marzano and colleagues analyzed research from over 100 studies on classroom management. They found that in classrooms where students had strong relationships with the teacher, there was a decrease in disruptions by 31 percent (Marzano, Marzano, & Pickering, 2003). We all know relationships take time. We'll cover relationships in a different chapter, but we wanted to point out that human connection can help your workload.

So, let's get to it. Here are ten questions for you to think about—your way of auditing your workload. Which aspects of your workload can you control?

| | STRONGLY AGREE | AGREE | SOMETIMES AGREE | DISAGREE |
|---|---|---|---|---|
| **There is a specific task that has added to my workload.** | 4 | 3 | 2 | 1 |
| **There are one or two students that drain time that I could spend with other students most days.** | 4 | 3 | 2 | 1 |
| **I get easily distracted during my prep period, which leads to spending more time after school completing tasks.** | 4 | 3 | 2 | 1 |
| **Compared to other teachers, I get things done so efficiently that admin comes to me with more tasks, which dramatically adds to my workload.** | 4 | 3 | 2 | 1 |
| **I don't spend as much time as I should planning engaging curriculum, which leads to more disengagement and behavior issues, which in turn adds to my workload (calling parents, etc.).** | 4 | 3 | 2 | 1 |

_____ **Average (Mean) Score**

**Score:**

16–20: If you have a mean score of 16–20, you definitely have many factors that are in your control that can decrease your workload. The good news is you can fix this, and you should! Look at areas where you rated yourself a 3 or 4. Be a hunter: Is there something you can do to solve this issue?

12–15: This is where most of us may be after a few years in the classroom. This score means you probably still have some frustration with your workload. The good news is you can fix it! Look at areas where you rated yourself a 3 or 4. Be a hunter: Is there something you can do to solve this issue?

8–11: Okay, we're impressed. Look at your highest score. What factors in your control can you change about this situation?

7 or below: Nicely done! You probably have time to build relationships with students and have spent time over the years hunting for ways to decrease your workload. Can you hunt a little more?

Take a few minutes to reflect on how you scored for each item. Use the questions below to guide your thinking or share with a friend or colleague.

## Your Turn

1. Ask other teachers how they handle their workload. (You'll know which ones to ask.)

2. Read and reflect on what others are writing about classroom workload. Even experts can learn from someone else.

STRATEGY #5

# Change Your Language Around Your Workload

## Be Positive and Optimistic

*Your Beliefs Become Your Thoughts*

*Your Thoughts Become Your Words*

*Your Words Become Your Actions*

*Your Actions Become Your Habits*

*Your Habits Become Your Values*

*Your Values Become Your Destiny*

*—Gandhi*

[Serena] I've done a lot of backpacking around the world. One of the biggest culture shocks occurs when I come back into the United States after a few weeks or even months being abroad. I hear the same phrase everywhere. It goes something like this:

> Me:      "Hey Juan, how are you doing? How has everything been?"
>
> Juan:      "Good—really busy but good."
>
> This is the accepted answer to show someone we are happy and successful. For some reason, we think that if we have a handle on all of our responsibilities, then maybe we aren't taking on enough or we have time and should be doing more work. Being stressed and busy is the norm. For some reason, the more exhausted we seem, the more it seems like we are accomplishing things. But why? Why is it often difficult to not take on more—to set time aside for ourselves, take a moment to smell the roses, and not be stressed? Why does it have to be like this? Let's flip the script:
>
> Me:      "Hey Juan, how are you doing? How has everything been?"
>
> Juan:      "Really good. I feel like I have a handle on everything at work and hopefully will soon have some free time to do more hiking with my family."

This response would probably shock you more. But let's change our mindset about our workload. This starts with our language. Let's listen to ourselves when we hear ourselves speak about our workload. This becomes our reality. It's okay to speak about your responsibilities with a sense of empowerment instead of a sense of defeat, even if you are speaking about the same workload. The purpose of this is explained in the quote that starts this chapter: Our words become our reality.

When we take control of our workload with our words and tone instead of rolling our eyes, our whole perception changes. You may even find yourself gravitating toward people who have the same mindset. If you truly are overwhelmed and stressed, then take something off your plate or create systems that make the load more efficient. We'll discuss how to do this in later chapters. Don't let stressed and busy become your accepted norm. You deserve better.

# Positive Thinking

On a deeper note, thinking positively takes it one more step. Kendra Cherry stated it perfectly in her 2018 article, "Understanding the Psychology of Positive Thinking," when she wrote,

> So what exactly is positive thinking? You might be tempted to assume that it implies seeing the world through rose-colored lenses by ignoring or glossing over the negative aspects of life. However, positive thinking actually means

*(Continued)*

(Continued)

approaching life's challenges with a positive outlook. It does not necessarily mean avoiding or ignoring the bad things; instead, it involves making the most of the potentially bad situations, trying to see the best in other people, and viewing yourself and your abilities in a positive light. (Cherry, 2018)

Why bother doing this? There are some very good reasons. According to the Mayo Clinic, positive thinking is linked to a wide range of health benefits, including the following:

▶ Longer life span

▶ Less stress

▶ Lower rates of depression

▶ Increased resistance to the common cold

▶ Better stress management and coping skills

▶ Lower risk of cardiovascular disease-related death

▶ Increased physical well-being

▶ Better psychological health (Cherry, 2018)

Even more interesting, research shows that if we *think* we can do a task, we actually have a much better chance of getting it done. Simply put, teachers who think they can, can. When we change our language around a task or workload, we change our mindset around that task or load. Our words become our reality.

If we want to go even deeper, self-efficacy (the belief that we can do something) has had powerful results for the classroom. In their 2016 study, published in the article "Teacher Self-Efficacy and Its Effects on Classroom Processes, Student Academic Adjustment, and Teacher Well-Being: A Synthesis of 40 Years of Research," Marjolein Zee and Helma M. Y. Koomen found that teachers with high self-efficacy:

▶ Have been demonstrated to perceive the implementation of new instructional methods as more important and congruent with their own practices

▶ Experience less self-survival, task, and impact concerns and more pedagogic conceptual change, irrespective of grade

▶ Effectively cope with a range of behaviors, regardless of grade

▶ Use proactive, student-centered classroom behavior strategies and practices

▶ Establish less conflictual relationships with students

▶ Become more sensitized to students' signals, needs, and expectations and thereby are able to provide students with adequate supports in class

It all starts with our words. Our words can change our mindset and belief system. When we start to take steps to control our workload and think positively at the same time, something magical happens. You'll start attracting teachers that have control of their workload and a sense of calm. Here are a few phrases you can practice saying to create a more positive mindset and gain more control of your workload.

Work has been piling up this week, but I'm working smarter and soon will have control over my load.

I've asked for some support because my responsibilities are too much for one person.

I'm excited about the proactive steps I've been taking in my classroom to make grading easier in the next unit.

Today I do feel defeated, but I know it's going to get better. I got this.

I actually feel great about how I've been managing my time in the classroom. I feel like I'm connecting to my students more, which is helping with classroom management and engagement.

Yes, okay, we get it. Some days you may just want to curl up into the fetal position after the last bell rings and cry. But no matter how much we have to do, we always have a choice about how we speak about our workload. Our words matter. The funny thing about people who don't think positively is that they call themselves realists. Nobody ever really calls themselves a pessimist. Don't fall for this. Optimists actually create their own reality. It's just brighter. Change your language; change how you feel.

## Your Turn

1. Think of a teacher or colleague who speaks positively and with a sense of empowerment about their workload. Have their words affected their reality?

2. Now think of a teacher or colleague who usually speaks negatively or with defeat about their workload. How do you think this has affected their teaching or relationships with students?

3. Which type of teacher do you want to be? Why?

# STRATEGY #6

# Am I Scraping the Right Car?

. . . . . . . . . . . . . . . . . . . . . . . . . . . . . . . . . . . . . . . . . . . . . . . . . . . . .

*Efficiency is doing things right; effectiveness is doing the right things.*

—*Peter Drucker*

There was once a Statoil commercial showing a man coming outside in the morning to find all of the cars on his street covered in snow. Approaching the car nearest his house, the man begins to painstakingly scrape snow off the windshield with his briefcase. He then clears off the side mirrors and, bracing himself against the cold, all four car windows. Despite the frigid temperature and slipping in the snow at least once, he even cleans off the windshield wipers with his gloved hands. Finally, he clicks his key fob to unlock the door only to find that the (still snow-covered) car in front of him is blinking its lights. He had spent an hour cleaning off the wrong car. You can watch *Cleaning Snow off the Wrong Car* on YouTube (Patel, 2013).

What would this misuse of time look like in the classroom? It could look like you spending way too much time on one student's behavior issues in class. This is not going to drive your entire class forward. It could also look like spending hours finding the perfect article to read in class when the article takes up only twenty minutes of your lesson. Sometimes it's okay to stop scraping because you are clearing the wrong car. It's just not worth it. Here is a mantra to help you. Ask yourself: "Am I scraping the right car?"

The bottom line is this: We decide how we use our time at school. To assess whether you are using your time wisely, remind yourself that your time should be spent on tasks that result in the following outcomes:

▶ Students are engaged and on task.

▶ We are continuing to grow as teachers.

▶ We are creating healthy bonds with colleagues and administrators.

▶ We are forming relationships with students.

▶ We are keeping communication open with parents.

▶ We are staying organized in our classrooms.

▶ We are prepping curriculum (making copies, writing notes on board, getting supply baskets ready, etc.)

▶ We are completing paperwork.

Figure 6.1 shows how your time spent should look.

**Figure 6.1** Ideal Allocation of Weekly Classroom Prep Time

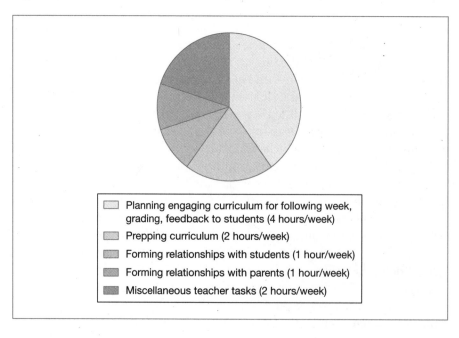

Try to get yourself ahead so most everything you are doing is proactive. You'll thank yourself later. It *is* possible. You are planning for the next week; using student data to inform instruction; sending a quick, positive e-mail to Amal's mom; planning your learning presentations; making copies for following week; and so on. Once you hit this, you have found your teaching stride. You are scraping the right car, and now you're using an ice scraper instead of just a credit card.

Here is a time-saver tip:

[Serena] If you dedicate more time to planning and being prepared to execute engaging curriculum, you will spend less time in long parent meetings. This is because, as you know from my first book, engaging and relevant curriculum is the mothership of classroom management. When you have better classroom management, your behavior issues start to disappear. Then you can focus one hour per week (max) on positive parent phone calls, positive parent e-mails, setting up parent volunteers, or quick in-person parent meetings.

## Your Turn

1. Have you ever spent way too much time "scraping the wrong car?" If so, describe what happened.

2. How do you know when this is happening?

3. What is a strategy you can use next time you are "scraping the wrong car?"

# STRATEGY #7

# Watch Your Water Cooler

*The higher your energy level, the more efficient your body. The more efficient your body, the better you feel and the more you will use your talent to produce outstanding results.*

—*Tony Robbins*

[Serena] The best analogy I can think of for energy is a water cooler. If you turn the knob and the water starts leaking, you have less water for later since there is a limited amount. The advice I can give for energy? Watch your water cooler; don't let too much water leak out unnecessarily. Be mindful about where you expend your energy.

Here are some energy leaks:

▶ Long, unneeded conversations about one student's repeated misbehavior

▶ Unhealthy food

▶ Lack of exercise

▶ Not enough water or sleep

▶ Complaining

▶ Facebook/social media

▶ Conversations with negative teachers or colleagues that seem to go in circles

▶ Taking student misbehaviors personally

▶ Responding to all e-mails immediately

▶ Overcommitting

▶ Multitasking

When we do these things during the school day, we are draining our energy. Then we have little energy to be productive when our prep time rolls around. You have so much talent. The trick is to make sure that you have enough energy to use your talent to the fullest.

Get organized about where you want to place your energy. Una Byrne, an independent consultant, published an article that explored the habits of effective time managers. She advised, "It is important that you have only *one* to-do list that works for you. It is amazing how much just writing things down lightens the burden and reduces the feeling of being overwhelmed" (2008, p. 192).

Here are a few other suggestions:

▶ Mindfully surround yourself with teachers who energize you. Carve out time to spend with them. These should be the teachers you spend the most time with.

▶ As much as possible, bring healthy lunches. Lunchtime will likely happen in a rush where you're just trying to get some fuel in; nutritious vegetables and energizing proteins will help get you through the rest of the day. Save delicious foods for dinner, when you have a bit more time to savor them.

▶ Keep healthy snacks in your desk so you are not tempted to buy nachos after school when you get the 3 p.m. munchies. High-protein snacks will keep your energy up. I always keep green tea packets in my desk drawer because green tea gives me pep without the coffee shakes. Do what works for you.

▶ Carve out only two to three times that you check and respond to e-mails throughout the day. Let your students' parents know that these are the times they can expect a response from you.

▶ If you feel that you are stuck in a draining conversation, it's okay to say you have to run to a meeting in five minutes. Or, if you *have* to have a conversation that you know will be draining, set up boundaries at the beginning. It could sound like this: "I'm so glad you called. I really want to talk to you, but I only have about ten minutes because I have to run to a meeting." Really, it's okay, because some people will talk as long as you let them. Setting boundaries helps manage expectations and provides you with a predetermined exit.

▶ If you've been asked to take on a task that you do not have the energy for, simply state, "I would love to help, but my plate is full right now." Your students will thank you. However, if you can help out, do! You may love the experience.

## Your Turn

1.  What is something you do during the school day that drains your energy? Can you think of another way to handle the situation? Can you avoid the situation in the future?

2.  What can you do when you find yourself in a situation where your energy is draining? How can you gracefully remove yourself from that situation?

3.  Which two times during the day can you commit to answering e-mails? Try this out for a week and take notice of whether this helps preserve your mental energy throughout the day.

STRATEGY
#8

# Get Unstuck When You Feel Paralyzed by Too Much to Do

*If you spend too much time thinking about a thing, you'll never get it done.*

—Bruce Lee

The title of this chapter may sound all too familiar to you. Think back to a time in your teaching career when you had a million and one little tasks to do and one daunting large task that you were putting off. You were probably putting it off because it was an unpleasant task. But as author Edward Young stated in 1742, "Procrastination is the thief of time."

Procrastination isn't so much about putting things off or forgetting; it's your brain's way of avoiding uncomfortable feelings or pain. However, the more we avoid a certain task, the more mental power it takes up in our head. The task probably isn't as annoying, frustrating, or painful as we make it out to be in our mind.

Chronically avoiding a necessary task is what we call being "stuck." You end up distracting yourself or keeping busy with minor tasks and then end the day feeling exhausted and more stressed about the big important task that still needs to get done. Our advice is to start the task in small increments.

Eventually you will complete it, and then you'll be able to spend your mental energy on other necessary tasks or enjoy some much-deserved stress-free relaxing time.

If procrastination seems to be more of a problem for you than it is for others, look for underlying issues. According to research conducted by Scott Taylor and colleagues, 75 percent of individuals with attention deficit hyperactivity disorder (ADHD) are classified as chronic procrastinators (Taylor, Chowdhury, & Pychyl, 2018; Pychyl, 2018). So, some of us may have it harder than others. Awareness is key.

# Strategies for Completing Tasks

## Tip #1: Prioritize

Stop doing the little tasks. Tackle the big important tasks first.

## Tip #2: Set a Visible Timer for Thirty or Sixty Minutes

Do that much each day. If you get interrupted (the phone rings, a student asks a question, etc.), stop the timer. Eventually, the task will get done. Kitchen timers work best because you will avoid the distractions of texts and social media that come with using cell phone or computer timers. The timer is a scaffold to help motivate you to gain momentum and keep a pace. After the time is up, you can add more time or stop. It's up to you. The bottom line is that you most likely took a huge chunk out of the task. After a few days, the task should be complete and you'll be unstuck.

## Tip #3: Remove Distractions

Do your best to eliminate distractions as you work on a task. Tips for doing this include the following:

▶ Shut your classroom door for an hour during your prep.

▶ Turn off e-mail notification alerts and silence your phone. Better yet, turn off your phone completely. Multitasking will hurt your chances of thinking critically.

▶ Beware of the "shiny new object" syndrome, especially on e-mail or texts. Stick with what you were doing from start to finish when possible.

## Tip #4: Set Aside and Move On

If you run into a roadblock, set that aspect of the task aside and move on to another aspect that can be done. Write down the roadblock issue to solve at a later time.

It is important to implement strategies to overcome procrastination to avoid the negative effects this behavior causes. Not only is procrastination the thief of time and of getting things done, it can also hurt our self-image and well-being. In a 2011 study of academic procrastination among college students, Laura Rabin, Joshua Fogel, and Katherine Nutter-Upham concluded that procrastination is self-regulation failure and leads to the following:

▶ Reduced agency

▶ Disorganization

▶ Poor impulse and emotional control

▶ Poor planning and goal setting

▶ Reduced use of metacognitive skills

▶ Poor task persistence

▶ Time and task management deficiencies (Pychyl, 2013)

Think of how much time and energy you could save by implementing some successful strategies to overcome procrastination. Try them out—you won't regret it.

## Your Turn

1. What high-priority task have you been putting off because you have little motivation or energy to do it?

2. Where can you complete this task with little chance of interruption? How can you alter your environment to decrease the chance of interruption?

3. How much time can you dedicate to biting off a large chunk of this task?

# STRATEGY #9

# Organize and Unclutter

*Teachers refuse to throw anything out because it might be useful in forty-seven years for that one art project.*

*—Jill Jackson, teacher and educational consultant*

[Ed] Serena and I were having coffee with a couple teachers we know, and we mentioned that we were working on Serena's second book on the topic of time management for teachers. We told them we were writing a section on how to unclutter your classroom. One of our friends asked if we had ever watched the Netflix series *Tidying Up With Marie Kondo*. Kondo is also the author of the best-selling book *The Life-Changing Magic of Tidying Up*. "You should start there," our friend told us.

Everybody seems to want to declutter their lives. Let's take a look at decluttering our classrooms. Kondo stresses that a person should consider every item in their home (or, in our case, their classroom). Organize by category. Forget nostalgia. Purge. Sentiment is not practical. Determine what is useful. Kondo's organizing philosophy is so effective that she was listed as one of *Time Magazine's* 100 Most Influential People of 2015. The KonMari method of organizing is based on categories:

▶ Clothing

▶ Books

‣ Papers

‣ Komono (miscellaneous items)

‣ Sentimental items

In many ways, your classroom is your one-room home with a bunch of kids running around it. We recommend that you use the following categories to organize your classroom:

‣ Your desk area: You need this area to be functional because this is where a lot of the magic happens. It is where you keep passes, student information, timers, confidential papers, etc. Start saving boxes to organize loose items inside of drawers. This will create a sense of visual peace when you look for something in your desk.

**Photo 9.1**

*Source:* eurobanks/iStock.com

‣ Student desks

‣ Books

‣ Stacks of papers: If your school has a scanner, perhaps you or a student can create an e-file so you have digital files of important papers rather than stacks of hard copies.

‣ Miscellaneous: Your students need a classroom that is organized, safe, clean, and easy to get around. Your classroom should be a pleasant and orderly place with uncluttered workspaces—a space that students will care about and take pride in.

[Ed] I remember a seventh-grade teacher, Barbara, whose classroom looked like a zoo. She saved everything. She was a classic hoarder. Near the end of the school year, other teachers would visit Barbara's room and negotiate with her about their supply needs. She sold off her supplies, charging them less than what they would pay in a store. This was the only time she decluttered her classroom each year.

Heather Wolpert-Gawron, author and teacher, wrote in her 2019 article about optimal learning environments that "the classroom environment is vital, and recent reports show that our rooms can have too much of a good thing. Posters, for example, might make a room feel inviting or engaging, but having too many can distract students." This advice is especially important if you teach cohort classes (classes with a high number of students with individualized education programs, or IEPs).

Here are a few ideas to declutter your classroom:

▶ First, take a breath, close your eyes, and ask yourself, "What would I like my classroom to look like?"

▶ Then, look around and ask yourself, "Why am I keeping this?" Do this after school, before school, or during your prep. It's best to do it when the students aren't around.

▶ Dedicate ten minutes twice a week (e.g., ten minutes every Tuesday and Thursday). Set a timer if you need that scaffold.

▶ Start with a section of your classroom.

▶ Papers usually account for a lot of classroom clutter.

▶ Use boxes to handle students' papers.

▶ Use boxes that are labeled (e.g., *units, lesson plans*).

▶ Involve students in your decluttering efforts.

▶ Spend some time visualizing what you want your classroom to look like.

▶ Donate the giveaways. Maybe one person on your teaching team can deliver the donations to a charity once per semester.

▶ Don't forget your desk drawers.

▶ Create a feedback box.

Here's an idea: Do the 4 × 4 Challenge! Every fourth week of each month, see if you can find items to throw away, recycle, relocate, or donate. Mark it on your calendar or, even better, schedule the activity with another teacher and hold each other accountable!

Allow yourself to have a designated place for clutter, out of student eyesight. This could be a filing cabinet, a closet, and so forth.

---

[Serena] In my office there's a tall filing cabinet that I just shove things into. It keeps clutter from other areas. People often think it's full of files. Nope—every drawer has stuff in it that doesn't have a home. The stuff ranges from extra sweaters in case I am chilly to a pair of running shoes to safety pins. I know where the stuff is, and it keeps my office looking neat and tidy and keeps me mentally organized. It works for me. The bottom line is that if you create an uncluttered and organized classroom, you will be a better teacher for your students.

---

We encourage you to ask yourself these questions when going through your things:

▶ Is this out of date? No longer of importance? The most recent copy?

▶ Do I have time to read/do something with this? How long have I told myself I would do something with it?

▶ Is there another resource if I get rid of this and need to revisit it later?

▶ What is the worst thing that would happen if I tossed this?

▶ Am I keeping this because I spent a lot of money on it? Am I getting any value out of it if it's not being used?

Perhaps you can have a student keep an eye on a part of the room to help you. For example, Skylar knows to straighten out the textbooks if they are a bit off, or Aiko knows to fix the poster if it comes down again. Remember, your students can take an active role in helping maintain their learning environment.

## Your Turn

1. Ask other teachers how they handle the clutter in their classrooms. We recommend you ask the teachers who don't have much (if any) clutter.

2. What ideas can you share about minimizing classroom clutter?

3. How can reducing classroom clutter help you become a more efficient teacher and also help your students learn more?

**STRATEGY #10**

# Prep Where It Counts Before the Start of School

....................................................

*Always focus on the front windshield and not the review mirror.*

—*Colin Powell*

Before the start of school, there is a window of opportunity where we can prep in areas where it counts to help us hit the ground running. Using these last few days before students return to school effectively can significantly affect the entire year in terms of time management, lower stress levels, more productivity, and more engaged and happy students.

[Serena] I didn't always know this. I completed my student teaching in an eighth-grade ELA classroom in a Native American boarding school. Luckily there were a few days before school started for teachers to set up their classrooms. I remember spending a big chunk of my time doing the task I was assigned— making a bulletin board featuring the first semester reading, *Harry Potter and the Sorcerer's Stone.* I was so excited. I laid out the colors and spent hours placing trivia questions under flaps of paper that students could use to quiz themselves on their Harry Potter knowledge. A neighboring student teacher even offered to help me. We were so proud of our finished purple creation and spent a few minutes smiling in our Potter glory. When the students arrived, they spent a few minutes flipping open the questions and then the excitement soon wore off. Looking back, I wish I had spent some of those hours planning with my master teacher and learning how to make engaging literacy curriculum. That year, we only planned week by week and were constantly flying by the seats of our pants to come up with engaging curriculum.

In my fifth year of teaching, I had a phenomenal co-teacher. Before school began, I used my first half-day organizing our classroom and doing anything but planning the first unit. During our first planning session before school, my co-teacher walked into my classroom and was ready to plan the first six-week unit. I thought, *What the heck? Why so early? Let's get to know the students first.* Despite my hesitation, we planned the unit in a week-by-week outline. We had a model final project trifold made, and we planned out the first week, day by day. Before the start of class, we had copies made for every class, separated by different colors of printer paper. Our parts where we would each lead instruction were marked on the lesson plans, and all that was left to do was the execution of the lesson. Our first week was engaging; the students were learning and we were relaxed and had fun with the lessons. We used our prep time to plan the next week's lessons. We were always one week ahead. We hit the ground running. Soon enough, we had extra time to do our bulletin board and even had a few students help. Prepping where it counted *before* day one with the students helped us stay one step ahead, which kept our stress level down and our productivity up all year long.

I'm not saying decorating a bulletin board or focusing on the aesthetics of a classroom is a waste of time for a teacher, but there are so many ways to use the prep time at the beginning of a school year more efficiently than spending hours hunting for Harry Potter trivia. In simpler terms, prepping where it counts can create long-lasting, systemic results to help your classroom run like a well-oiled machine and give you more time during the school year.

Here's some practical advice that can help as a roadmap.

*Before the start of day one:*

▶ Plan your first unit.

▶ Set up your Google Classroom (or other digital platform) with student names from your roster.

▶ Set up your gradebook with student names.

▶ Set up your classroom behavior modification system (if applicable).

▶ Have lunch/coffee with your co-teacher to start forming a strong relationship before the students come. This will help immensely with communication down the line.

▶ Have copies made for your first week of school. Note: Expect the school copier to break in the first week because every other teacher will also be making copies. Plan early to avoid stress and wasted time waiting in line.

▶ Set up a Donors Choose for your classroom to get materials donated for future units.

▶ Have your sign-in/sign-out sheet ready for classroom technology.

▶ Have your class website up and ready.

*Do not spend **much** time on:*

▶ Bulletin boards. You can even start the school year with empty bulletin boards that have a simple and nice background. Student work can go on the bulletin boards as the year progresses.

▶ Door decorations. You'll have time for this later.

The ratio I like to use is two thirds to one third. For at least the first few weeks, two thirds of your prep time before the start of school should be related to setting up the academics of the classroom, making it logistically functional, and getting the curriculum ready and prepped. One third of the prep time can be for décor, relationship building, and making everything look nice.

Let's get real about why prepping where it counts in the beginning of the year matters. Research suggests that "planning decisions made early in the academic year exert a profound influence on teachers' planning for the remainder of the year" (Shavelson, 1981, p. 479). Simply stated, the amount of time we dedicate to being proactive with the academic side of our classroom pays off big time in the end by saving us from stress and loss of energy. Unfortunately, the amount of time we spend on aesthetics and other aspects of the classroom may not have such a direct payoff to our personal well-being.

Where and how we decide to use our time before the first days of school can have a huge impact on our energy and stress levels midway through the year.

# Your Turn

1.  Reflect: How did you spend your time prepping before day one in past years? How did this affect your stress level, engagement, and classroom management throughout those years?

2.  What are your thoughts on the one third–two thirds rule to prepping before day one? Do you think this will work for your classroom?

3.  What part of the academics of your classroom can you start prepping before day one?

# PART II

## PLANNING

Illustration by Paper Scraps Inc.

*When I was a new teacher in the middle school resource room, the principal came in and I had run out of my lesson (poor planning) and we were just sitting around. The principal had his pen and pad. I told the kids to come with me behind the dividers and we sneaked out of the room, leaving him there. Later he asked where I had gone. I don't remember what I told him, but I did invite him back to observe again!*

—Ellen, retired high school teacher in Maine

# Cut Down
# Your Grading Time

*A policeman pulled me over and asked for my papers. I gladly gave him all of my students' essays and drove off.*

*—Heidi McDonald*

[Serena] Like most teachers, I had a lot of students. I taught over 120 eighth-grade students every day. Not only do we already have a significant number of students to teach and manage but the numbers seem to be growing. This means heaps of grading and even more feedback to ensure truly effective learning. The problem is that we are just one person tasked with these work-loads. The biggest time management issue with grading is that we usually don't have the time to give the amount of feedback we'd like for each student, and if we *do* try to take that time, we come to school the next day so drained we can't effectively execute a lesson.

Let's say a teacher who has 100 students spends five minutes grading each final project— optimistically speaking, of course. That's over ten hours of grading. And this estimation does not account for any feedback along the way, and it definitely doesn't account for follow-up submissions, which can double the required time.

# Promoting a More Comprehensive Learning Process Can Reduce Grading Time

Teach your students how to peer conference each other's work a few times throughout the construction period before they submit the work to you for final grading. This should be a class activity you all do together. Students could even meet with two different peers. (Everybody participates if they have at least half of the assignment finished.) The secret is to show them how to do it. This could set you up for the rest of the year because you can repeat the process with each major assignment. The first time you introduce peer review, model it for your students with another teacher or a student partner. Prepare a rubric ahead of time that students work from when evaluating the work of their peers. The rubric can become more detailed or contain more items as the assignment develops over time. Figures 11.1 and 11.2 provide examples of how the rubrics for peer reviewing could look different in three peer review sessions, each a few days apart.

In an English classroom, the final peer review would be done with the same rubric the teacher uses for grading. The teacher would also provide a space on the rubric where the students could give each other constructive feedback, praise, and suggestions for edits/revisions. The session before that could be checklists that have parts of the final rubric since students are building their persuasive essays with time.

**Figure 11.1** Sample of a Rubric for a Beginning Peer-to-Peer Conference for a Persuasive Essay

| SCORE | 4 | 3 | 2 | 1 |
|---|---|---|---|---|
| VOICE | Sounds confident, convincing, and compelling<br><br>Reactions and feelings are well stated<br><br>Uses formal writing that is mature | Sounds confident<br><br>Reactions and feelings are clear<br><br>Uses formal writing that is grade-level appropriate | Attempts to sound confident<br><br>Reactions and feelings are somewhat well stated<br><br>Writes informally | Unclear sense of audience and purpose |

*(Continued)*

**Figure 11.1**    (Continued)

| SCORE | 4 | 3 | 2 | 1 |
|---|---|---|---|---|
| WORD CHOICE | Uses powerful, compelling words throughout the entire essay | Uses powerful, compelling words in most of the essay | Attempts to use powerful and compelling words in the essay | Limited vocabulary<br><br>Words used incorrectly |
| STRUCTURE | Purposeful and powerful sentence structure<br><br>Effective use of signal transition words and quotations that support the ideas in the essay | Strong sentence structure<br><br>Clear use of signal transition words and quotations that support the ideas in the essay | Weak sentence structure<br><br>Attempts to use signal transition words and quotations that support the ideas in the essay | Little or no sense of sentence structure |
| CONVENTIONS | Free of errors in quotation mark usage and citations<br><br>Free of errors in comma usage<br><br>Punctuates names of books and texts correctly<br><br>Free of errors in spelling and grammar | Minor errors in quotation mark usage and citations<br><br>Minor errors in comma usage<br><br>Punctuates names of books and texts correctly<br><br>Minor errors in spelling and grammar | Many errors in quotation mark usage and citations<br><br>Many errors in comma usage<br><br>Attempts to punctuate names of books and texts correctly<br><br>Many errors in spelling and grammar | Limited understanding of grade-appropriate spelling, grammar, and punctuation |

Areas of strength:

Areas of growth:

Additional comments:

**Figure 11.2**   Peer–Peer Conference Rubric

## Persuasive Essay

**My partner's persuasive essay . . . (check all that apply)**

| YES | NO | **VOICE** |
|-----|-----|-----------|
| | | Sounds confident |
| | | Uses formal language |
| | | Reactions and feelings are well stated |

Comments (suggestions, praise, room for improvement)

| YES | NO | **WORD CHOICE** |
|-----|-----|-----------------|
| | | Uses powerful and compelling language |

Comments (suggestions, praise, room for improvement)

| YES | NO | **STRUCTURE** |
|-----|-----|---------------|
| | | Has purposeful and powerful sentence structure |
| | | Uses transition words effectively |
| | | Uses quotations that clearly support the author |

Comments (suggestions, praise, room for improvement)

| YES | NO | **CONVENTIONS** |
|-----|-----|-----------------|
| | | Uses quotation marks correctly |
| | | Uses commas correctly |
| | | Uses punctuation in book titles correctly |
| | | Uses correct spelling and grammar |

Comments (suggestions, praise, room for improvement)

Here are some key elements of peer review:

> **Written feedback.** The peer reviewer should write down what the student needs to revise. Written feedback is key to improvement in subsequent drafts or iterations of a project.

> **Time to revise based on feedback.** Immediately after the peer review session, while class is still in session, give the student time to make revisions on the evaluated work. This is crucial.

> **Peer reviewers act as experts.** Instruct the peer reviewers to offer feedback as if they were the teacher. Reviewers should identify positive aspects of the work (write these down) as well as indicate where the student can make improvements.

Feedback is one of the most powerful tools of learning. According to an October 2018 report listing 250 influences on student achievement culled from 1,500 meta-analyses of 90,000 studies involving 300 million students, feedback was rated as a factor that would "considerably raise student achievement" (Hattie, 2018). The more constructive (and informed) feedback students get, whether it comes from you or their classmates, the better.

A mini-lesson on the benefits of respectful, constructive feedback is very helpful in modeling this peer review process. The short video *Austin's Butterfly* is a cute and clever way to illustrate to students how specific peer feedback can increase learning, create a community of learners, and produce more solid final products. Scan the QR code for Video 11.1 to watch Austin's progress. Showing the video to your class is an enjoyable and informative way to launch the first peer editing session.

Peer reviews represent an *easier* and very powerful way to cut down on time spent on the grading process without skimping on the care, thoughtful teacher feedback, and attention your students truly deserve. It's simple and benefits the class in many ways, such as the following:

> It will cut down on your grading time because you will *receive higher quality work* at submission time.

> It will create a community of learners in your classroom and students will *gain trust* in each other.

> Students will *understand* the project expectations and rubric more thoroughly as they check each other's work.

Video 11.1
*Feedback: Building Excellence in Student Work*

To read a QR code, you must have a smartphone or tablet with a camera. We recommend that you download a QR code reader app that is made specifically for your phone or tablet brand.

▶ By evaluating the work of others and offering feedback, students will become better able to evaluate and improve their own work. Remember from Bloom's taxonomy that evaluation is critical thinking.

▶ Your final grade will be given to a higher-quality assignment and you will be able to give more constructive feedback.

▶ Students will become more independent learners.

Do this a few times and you and your class will be hooked. It can work for any discipline and any grade level. I've done peer conferencing with elementary students all the way up to high school seniors. This practice creates independent learners who will be ready to turn in their best efforts with the help of their peers. Using a system like this will not only save you time on grading but will also help the students produce higher-quality work without your assistance.

Another idea to manage your grading time comes from Catlin Tucker, the Sonoma County 2010 teacher of the year. According to Tucker, "If students are working on an essay, I dedicate one station each day to providing real-time feedback as they write. I meet with individual students. These grading conversations take about 3 minutes because I do *not* try to grade every single aspect of their paper or assignment. Instead, I select 2–3 specific skills to assess for a score" (2017).

Managing your grading time by doing some of the grading in class, whether it be peer–peer or student–teacher assessment, also increases connections in your classroom, creates a community of learners that help and support one another, and gives us that extra time on nights and weekends to spend recharging our own precious batteries.

## Your Turn

1. Do you think peer review would work for your class? Why or why not?

2. What other time savers have you found that have cut down on grading time?

3. Talk to your fellow teachers and ask them what time-saving devices they use regarding grading. Did you find any new practices that you might want to implement in your own classroom?

4. What value do you see in creating a community of learners in order to decrease your grading time and get higher-quality student work? How feasible do you think this is?

# Meetings

## Stick to an Agenda to Save Time

> *If you had to identify, in one word, the reason why the human race has not achieved, and never will achieve, its full potential, that word would be "meetings."*
>
> —*Dave Barry*

Dave Barry is referring to meetings that drone on and on. We're not talking about those types of meetings. We've seen meetings done well that produced powerful results. Meetings can drive initiatives forward, make lessons come to life, and solve complex issues in school. Most effective meetings use agendas.

[Serena] In my experience, groups of teachers in teacher meetings often do not complete the task they set out to do. Why? Because teachers just *love* talking about what Melissa did in science class, or how Booker stuck his slime under the table. Teachers rarely get to talk to each other, and it's just plain fun to share stories with each other. I get it.

The problem is that as fun and stress relieving as it is to laugh with your colleagues about how José said the funniest thing again in art class, your units have to get made, IEP meetings need to take place, and logistics for the upcoming field trip need to be finalized.

There are two types of meetings—the formal meeting and the informal meeting.

# Formal Meetings

Characteristics of formal meetings are as follows:

▶ These meetings are called for a specific purpose.

▶ Such meetings are scheduled for specific recurring dates and times to keep forward momentum in a team or organization. For these types of formal meetings, we recommend that each meeting be limited to no more than an hour and a half.

▶ An agenda is prepared and distributed for each meeting.

▶ Minutes are taken, noting essential discussion points, recommendations, and decisions reached.

## Agendas for Formal Meetings

An agenda for a formal meeting serves the following purposes:

▶ It identifies the items (problems, issues, changes) that need to be discussed. Therefore, the agenda answers the question "Why are we meeting?"

▶ It determines the order in which items will be discussed and how much time should be spent discussing each item.

▶ An agenda distributed before the day of the meeting suggests ways committee members can prepare by gathering their thoughts (and perhaps data) on the discussion points ahead of time. Participants who come prepared will feel more at ease.

▶ It helps keep the chairperson on task and on schedule.

▶ It empowers individual members by serving as an invitation for each member to bring her or his ideas and concerns to the meeting.

▶ It provides a base for developing future agendas.

▶ It offers a way to determine the success of the meeting and whether future meetings will be needed.

At the conclusion of a productive formal meeting, the chair and committee members should agree on what actions are necessary and assign who is responsible for each action. In some cases, an action item might be to create a subcommittee of other people with a current committee member serving as the chair for the new subcommittee.

# Informal Meetings

Characteristics of informal meetings are as follows:

▶ Informal meetings are called for a specific purpose.

▶ Such meetings often are the result of an issue or problem.

▶ Agendas may or may not be appropriate for the meeting.

Informal meetings address what is on the mind of people you work with who want to talk about issues, practices, events, behaviors, celebrations, and so on.

[Ed] One Saturday after Thanksgiving while I was school principal, I invited any school personnel who wanted to work out to come to the school gym. Several people showed up, including four teachers. We played basketball. On a break, two teachers approached me (informal meeting) to express their concern about the last three months of school with the caveat, "You know Ed, we have to do something about turning the kids on in this school."

Although I had already planned the agenda for the faculty meeting scheduled for the first week in December (just a few days away), I changed the agenda after some consultation with others. The agenda listed the meeting day and time and the room where we would meet. It also included the following statement: "We have one discussion item. I would like you to help us answer this question: What should we be doing in the New Year to turn kids on in this school?"

The staff came with their ideas, and we had a brainstorming session for about thirty minutes. Shirley, our English teacher, wrote down all of the suggestions on the blackboard. The staff generated a list of about fifteen to twenty ideas. Shirley then led us in prioritizing the list. Another teacher came up with the idea that we should do something that would surprise the kids when they came back in January.

About eleventh on the list was this idea: Use daily newspapers. Alice, our reading teacher, said, "I have an idea. Why don't we tell the students on their first day back that we have put away the textbooks? No textbooks for

*(Continued)*

(Continued)

two weeks. We are going to use our local and state newspapers for the next two weeks with each student and teacher getting a copy of both." After some discussion, the teachers agreed. They left it to me to get the newspapers. They also agreed that they would try to come in a half hour earlier each day to cooperatively plan lessons and newspaper projects.

Not only did our curriculum change but so did the attitudes, enthusiasm, and creativity of the teachers and students. Daily attendance improved. We saw greater support and involvement from parents (the students took the newspapers home with them each day). That meeting containing one agenda item resulted in my teachers feeling empowered and that their time was valued, and they were filled with a sense of accomplishment.

# Your Turn

1. Take a day or two as you go about your regular school day and take note of how many informal meetings you and others have. Limit your list only to meetings in which the discussions are about school matters and issues.

2. Try using an agenda for your next formal meeting or ask if you can write an agenda for the next meeting if you are not the chair.

# STRATEGY #13

# What's Your Right Climate?

*I like it 72 degrees, with a slight wind blowing to the north, and a 45 percent moisture index in order to do my optimal grading.*

—*Anonymous teacher*

We spend hours upon end to make sure our classrooms are comfortable, inviting, clean, and optimal for student learning. We know as teachers that students will learn better and be able to work more efficiently if we create the right environment. But do we give that same amount of attention to the environment where we create our lesson plans or do other important critical thinking? Let's give the same amount of love to ourselves. You deserve it.

The important factor to remember is this: You have control over the environment you work in. A messy desk equals messy thinking. A cold teacher will not be as creative as a warm teacher. Temperature matters, an organized work space matters, lighting matters, and a clean workspace matters. You deserve this as much as your students. Often during the school year we give more time and attention to our students than to ourselves. We challenge you to flip the script and take a second to visualize a workspace that would be optimal for creating engaging lesson plans.

1.  **How important is temperature for your comfort level?**

    *Not important*          *Somewhat important*          *Very important*

2.  **What type of background noise or music do you need to stay focused?**

    _____

3.  **What type of seating makes you the most focused?**

    *A comfy couch*          *A desk*          *Bed*          *Other*

4.  **What type of lighting do you need for your optimal thinking/ concentration?**

    *Natural lighting*     *Soft desk lamp*     *Office/classroom lighting*     *Does not matter*

5.  **Where do you often do your grading or lesson plan creation?**

    _____

Now let's compare. Is the place where you create your lesson plans optimal to *your* right climate? If it is, wonderful! If not, what can you change? Can you change something about your working environment, or do you need to work in a different location?

## Your Turn

1.  Where do you do most of your work that requires a high level of cognition?

2.  Based on the questions above, is this the best place for you to work? Why or why not?

3.  What factors can you add or remove from your environment to help you focus more and be more efficient in this environment?

**STRATEGY #14**

# Be Proactive, Not Reactive With Tasks

During my first year as a teacher, I watched veteran teacher Alex to learn how he (seemingly effortlessly) managed his time. Alex was a "stickler" on four things. He actually had me write them down:

1. Work hard (be proactive) on developing relationships with students' parents and your colleagues here in the school. You'll need the support at some point in the school year.

2. Plan your units and lessons carefully; design them to engage students.

3. Remember you are part of a team—a team built on trust, positive relationships, and caring for one another. Be accountable.

4. Lastly, make your "mark"—be proactive; don't whine; pull your weight; help empower those who work with you; share your skills, interest, and talents with others; and be a good communicator (listen, share, participate).

Four strategies for being proactive follow.

1. **Be strategic when asking for help from others.** At some point you will need to ask for help from someone, you will need someone to fix something, or you will need to borrow something from someone. When you realize this need, write the need and the person's name down on a sticky note. Chances

are, that person will pop into your room during the day. When they do, go over to your sticky-posting area and grab the sticky with that person's name on it to remind yourself what you need to ask them. This accomplishes two things: It helps you organize your thoughts and needs, and writing this information down frees your mind to focus on your class instead of a running to-do list in your head. You'll also save time by not having to chase the person down if you are able to instead take advantage of them dropping in for a quick visit. If you *do* end up seeking that person out for a walk or a chat, take the sticky with you so that you don't forget what you want to ask them.

2. **Make daily to-do lists.** Divide them into three categories:

▶ Do today

▶ Do tomorrow

▶ Do later this week

Be proactive in how you manage your out-of-school activities and responsibilities. Take care of them before they become a crisis.

3. **Practice self-care.** Be proactive in taking care of yourself before it results in weight gain, unmanageable stress, and daily fatigue. This means making healthy choices about exercise, mindfulness, and diet. Cultivate a positive mindset. Abraham Lincoln wrote, "Most folks are about as happy as they make up their minds to be."

4. **Practice mindfulness.** Develop skills that help you recognize and reflect on your reactions to certain situations. Learn how to direct yourself away from actions that are detrimental to yourself and those around you.

# Your Turn

1.  Which strategy for being proactive stands out most for you?

2.  How would you rate yourself on a proactive–reactive scale? Does your rating depend on the circumstances?

3.  Which of these strategies would you share with your students and colleagues?

# Cell Phones, E-mails, and Social Media . . . Oh My!

*We're surrounded by distractions. Whether it's e-mails, phone calls, text messages, social media notifications, or people entering and leaving your workspace, those distractions end up eating a good portion of your time.*

*—John Rampton, entrepreneur, investor, and online marketing guru*

[Serena] When I upgraded recently to a new computer, I noticed that my Facebook notifications would pop up over my Word documents. This same type of social media distraction occurred when I downloaded Facebook messenger and Twitter on my phone in order to connect with my international friends. If Joe Smith from Iowa wanted me to subscribe to his online newsletter, a *ding* would interrupt a lesson-planning session. While I was teaching, if I reached for my phone to set a timer or use another tool, I would see unimportant message alerts popping up, distracting me from the task at hand. I had to be proactive in changing the default settings on my phone and computer to remove non-essential pop-up messages. Our students are facing these same distractions. When we ask them to turn off their phones to focus on homework, they usually respond, "But I can multitask! It helps me relax and focus if my phone is on." But multitasking doesn't work.

In 2015 three researchers—Lin Lin, Deborah Cockerham, and Zhengsi Chang—conducted a study investigating the multitasking abilities of 168 participants, ages six to seventy-two, by measuring their task accuracy and completion time when they completed a visual or auditory task alone (single-tasking) compared to when they attempted the two tasks simultaneously (multitasking). The study found that

> neither the male nor the female participants showed an overall ability to excel in multitasking, but differences between age groupings were statistically significant. Teenagers (ages 13–19) and young adults (ages 20–40) not only spoke of confidence in their own multitasking abilities, but also earned the fastest, most accurate scores. Results showed significantly lower accuracy and completion time. (Lin, Cockerham, & Chang, 2015)

The data did reveal that children and young adults are more effective multitaskers than those of us over forty. However, "Of the 168 participants in [the] study, only 7 were faster at multitasking than at single-tasking" (Lin et al., 2015). Which proves that even if young people *are* more effective at multitasking than their elders, almost all of us are more productive when we focus on one single task, regardless of our age. The bottom line is that if you or your students multitask, it's probably going to take longer to complete the task, and you will more than likely make at least a few mistakes.

## We All Work Faster Without Social Media Distractions

The 2015 study also tested task accuracy with auditory distractions. The researchers found that "the majority of the participants (96%) performed faster and more accurately [when counting the shapes] in the single-tasking condition than in the multi-tasking condition" (Lin et al., 2015). Chances are we'd all be able to complete tasks more accurately with less auditory distractions, such as chimes from our computers and phones alerting us to new messages. We have the power to control our own well-being by turning these notifications off.

Some tasks require more time and accuracy than others. For example:

▶ Lesson planning

▶ Student feedback

▶ Conferencing with students

▶ Teaching a lesson

▶ Meetings

Protect your well-being by limiting your distractions as much as possible while you are completing these tasks.

Another landmark study analyzing multitasking was conducted at the Institute of Psychiatry at the University of London. This study focused on 1,100 office workers in a British company. It was concluded that multitasking actually temporarily lowers your IQ more than smoking marijuana or losing a night's sleep.

## Attention Residue

Sophie Leroy, a business professor at the University of Minnesota, coined the term *attention residue* in her 2009 article "Why Is It So Hard to Do My Work?" Simply put, our productivity suffers when we switch from one task to another and back again. However, Leroy admits, "Going from one meeting to the next, starting to work on one project and soon after having to transition to another is just part of life in organizations" (2009). Cal Newport mentioned Leroy's publication in his book *Deep Work* as he explained further,

> It might seem harmless to take a quick glance at your inbox every ten minutes or so. Indeed, many justify this behavior as better than the old practice of leaving an inbox open on the screen at all times (a straw-man habit that few follow anymore). But Leroy teaches us that this is not in fact much of an improvement. That quick check introduces a new target for your attention. Even worse, by seeing messages that you cannot deal with at the moment (which is almost always the case), you'll be forced to turn back to the primary task with a secondary task left unfinished. (Newport, 2016, p. 43)

What does this mean for you? You'll go back to your lesson clouded, or go into a student conference mentally distracted. We suggest you pick times to check your e-mail and commit to not checking outside of those times. If you set aside times when you can answer e-mails with thought and clarity, the recipients will appreciate your responses much more than if you answer hastily. Times for optimal attention are before school, during lunch, and during your prep.

## Your Turn

1. What times during the day could you block off for e-mails? How much time would you limit yourself to?

2. Think of a time you focused on one activity from start to finish. How did the product turn out?

3. Do you receive social media notifications on your phone and computer? Can you remove those notifications now to help you complete tasks faster and more accurately so you have time for real connection later?

# STRATEGY #16

# Plan Enough Time for Each Student

. . . . . . . . . . . . . . . . . . . . . . . . . . . . . . . . . . . . . . . . . . . . . . . . . . . . . . . . . . . . . . . . . . .

*Teacher [kindly asks student]: Aurelia, how much time and attention do you need from me?*

*Aurelia: All of it.*

Do any of you have Aurelias in your classroom? We bet you do. In a 2019 Edutopia article titled "The Biggest Lesson of My First Year Teaching," Cindy Bourdo described her quest to figure out why some teachers seemed to "have it easier" than others. She wrote,

> I looked around and saw that there were some teachers who seemed to just take everything in stride and really enjoyed what they were doing. Their classrooms ran smoothly, and their students looked happy. Over a few months, I observed these teachers . . . I started to see that the highest priority for these teachers was forming relationships with these students— everything else fell into place after that. (Bourdo, 2019)

As mentioned in Strategy #4, after analyzing more than 100 studies on classroom management, Robert Marzano and colleagues concluded that in classrooms where students had strong relationships with the teacher, there was a decrease in disruptions by 31 percent (Marzano et al., 2003). Fewer discipline issues means more time. Planning enough time for each student does not necessarily mean that you connect 1:1 with all 150 of your students on a deep level every day. You would have to multiply yourself by ten. What it *does* mean is that your classroom is set up so that students are heard and valued and their voices are celebrated daily. They are seen as human beings, not just students. Their unique personalities and skills are appreciated and recognized.

So how do we make enough time for each student? Here are eight ideas that will help you save time in your classroom and connect with your students on a human level. We suggest you try at least one per week. You will most likely find yourself combining a few or doing more than one once you get started.

# 1. Morning Meetings and Restorative Circles

## Morning Meetings/Dialogue Circles

There is a great deal of literature on different types of K–12 circle meetings, but the idea is always the same: Bringing students together as a whole class can help the teacher connect with the students as well as foster student-to-student connection and create a safe space where voices are heard and recognized.

During morning meetings teachers can check in and connect with students in a nonacademic way. Usually there is a greeting and some sort of short conversation piece regarding a quote or a current event, or there may be a brief character- or team-building activity. The point is that you want to get students talking to each other and to you because that's how human beings form bonds. Sometimes the teacher may go over announcements. The morning meeting sets a tone and launches the learning for the day. We've also seen these types of meetings close out the week. Although morning meetings or dialogue circles can look different from one classroom or grade to another, there are common best practices that you will find in all of them:

- Teacher and students sit in a circle and everyone participates.

- Students and teacher take turns talking.

- A safe space is formed to guide students into the learning of the day.

These dialogue circles can be a daily or weekly practice as a proactive approach to connect and check in with students and build a community of learners.

Companies and institutions often use dialogue circles at the beginning of meetings to make sure members of the group feel valued, to check in before

Video 16.1:
*Using Dialogue
Circles to Support
Classroom
Management*

business starts, and to get ready for what is to come. Scan the QR code for Video 16.1 to hear elementary teacher Edwina Smith talk about the benefits of dialogue circles and to see those circles in action.

Dialogue circles give your students the chance to see that you care about them as human beings, and they foster a sense of belonging with the class. It might be hard to believe at first, but taking the time to have a dialogue circle can save time overall. For those of you who feel most pressed for time, consider doing a check-in circle on Monday and a check-out circle on Friday. For elementary, middle, and younger high school students, we suggest you use a talking piece at least in the beginning of the year as a scaffold to teach listening skills. Only the person holding the talking piece is allowed to talk. No interruptions.

Dialogue circles give you a few minutes of connection with students every week or even daily. Students are creatures of habit, so if you start the school year out doing the circles regularly, they will become part of your classroom culture. As the year progresses, we suggest having students lead them. Not only is this an empowering practice for students but it can also give you a quick mental break as you listen rather than lead. A typical morning meeting can take as little as ten minutes, especially if you start class with your students already in a circle.

## Restorative Circles

Video 16.2:
*Restorative
Circles: Creating a
Safe Environment
for Students to
Reflect*

Similar to dialogue circles, restorative circles also help build stronger relationships between students. The biggest difference is that restorative circles often address an issue that has come up or something students did. The purpose of the restorative circle is to repair harm that has been done. Restorative circles can be done with the whole class or only with the individuals involved in the incident. Restorative circles occur when needed and are a reactive approach to restoring peace when something has been said or done that needs to be addressed. Scan QR code 16.2 to hear students and teachers talk about the practice of restorative circles at Pearl-Cohn High School.

## 2. Use Student Names

Know students' names and nicknames. Seating charts can help during the first days of class when you are still learning names. Use students' names when giving direction as much as possible in the beginning of the school year. The more you use your students' names, the faster you will learn them. If a student has a nickname they prefer, they will tell you.

**Figure 16.1**   Features of Dialogue Meetings and Restorative Circles

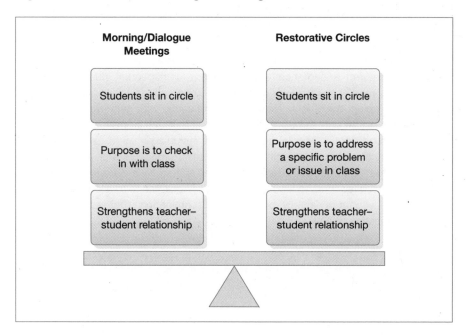

[Serena] I used to write student nicknames on my seating chart. I had one student who asked me to call him a shortened version of his name on day one. The fact that I jotted it down and remembered every time he was called on in class helped him feel like I understood him. A person's name is their favorite word. Remember that.

## A Note About Student Pronouns and Gender Identity

Our schools are becoming more welcoming places for students who express diverse gender identities. As teachers we have the responsibility of respecting students' preferred gender pronouns and the gender identities of transgender and nonbinary individuals. It's important that you ensure there is a caring community of learners within your class if a student asks to be referred to by a particular gender pronoun. Your school counselor or psychologist is a useful resource to go to in navigating these discussions with your classroom.

We interviewed Dr. Joseph Pariser, assistant professor of urology at the University of Minnesota, who specializes in transgender surgery, about this topic. According to him,

> With increasing acceptance and awareness, transgender students may transition socially much earlier than previous generations. While children are still developing, transitioning can help significantly with gender dysphoria, the distress that comes between the mismatch of one's physical body and their gender identity. Mental health issues, including suicide, are rampant in the transgender community, which stems from dysphoria and social acceptance. A student's preferred pronouns should always be used. There is an onus on teachers to lead a classroom of acceptance to allow students to thrive without a fear of bullying or discrimination. (Pariser, personal communication, 2019)

As teachers, we lead by example with our words and actions.

## 3. Quote Chat

As the class arrives, engage students by giving them a question or quote for the day. Have them work in pairs for just a few minutes. Quotes can be an inspirational way to set the tone for your lesson and get students talking to one another. If you can relate the quote to what you are teaching, that's where the magic happens. Hearing students' responses allows you to connect with them on a non-threatening academic level and build connection before the formal lesson begins.

## 4. Celebrations

Assign student groups to take the lead in how certain calendar holidays and special event days might be celebrated in class. We recommend you limit it to one or two events per month; for example, Martin Luther King, Jr. Day in January and Presidents' Day in February.

It is equally important to find ways to celebrate student successes. Organizations often have committees that celebrate people's birthdays and shout out accomplishments during the weekly or monthly company meeting. You can ask two or three students to be on the Celebration Committee for each of your classes. This committee can keep track of birthdays and shout-outs (e.g., Roberto made the soccer team this week) and keep a celebration/shout-out board in the classroom that students contribute to. Google Forms is one easy way for students to submit upcoming birthdays and accomplishments that can be tracked by the Celebration Committee and announced during the weekly dialogue circle.

Classrooms where students are given leadership opportunities and forums to celebrate each other's accomplishments are classrooms that nurture a strong community of learners who feel cared for as well as safe and supported by one another.

## 5. Enhance Your Classroom Climate—Delegate!

It's the students' classroom as much as it is yours. If you really want to know your students, give them responsibilities for leading and managing classroom matters and utilize their strengths so they shine. But be patient. They have to learn a range of skills like planning, solving problems, goal setting, and decision making when taking on leadership positions in your classroom. Be careful not to default to "It's easier if I just do it." If you teach students how to do something, praise them often to help them learn faster. An example of a responsibility you can delegate might be letting students supervise library book sign-outs or letting a student lead a portion of your morning meeting. Time management–wise it's a win-win situation for you since it's one less responsibility you have to manage. When you give students responsibilities, you are teaching them lifelong skills and you are benefiting from their perspectives and suggestions for creating a positive classroom culture. Delegating responsibilities and promoting student leadership skills will result in increased student satisfaction, better communication, and increased collaboration. You might also see students improve in their ability to set goals and manage conflict, and their resilience may increase. For further ideas on student leadership—for example, in peer mediation—see Strategy #17.

## 6. Hold Group Conferences

Student can get more individualized attention from each other as well as from you. Reading conferences are a good way for students to engage in discussions of literature with you and one or two peers. Meet with two to three students who are reading books in similar genres. These types of small conferences are especially helpful for English learners who might experience anxiety in 1:1 meetings with the teacher or who may be reticent to talk in large groups. Having a conversation with peers lessens the pressure and may make them more confident in sharing their thoughts.

# 7. "Get to Know Me" Activities

In her 2019 Edutopia article, Cindy Bourdo, the first-year teacher described at the beginning of this chapter, shared a short game called Who Is It? According to her, "Each student writes two to three unique things about themselves on a sticky note with their name. I collect the notes and read them to the class, and they have to guess who wrote it" (Bourdo, 2019). In a very short amount of time, this game allows students to get to know each other better. It is especially beneficial for quieter students. Playing the game communicates to students that you want to get to know them as individuals. Also, it's interactive and much more fun than filling out an "About Me" worksheet. Activities such as this should take three to five minutes, max.

# 8. Family Boards

Have a spot in your room dedicated to pictures of your students working, presenting their work, or just being themselves and having fun. It's important to show both types of pictures. Photo displays honoring your students shows them you care. Students love taking ownership of the "family board" or "wall of fame." I prefer hard copy pictures hung in the classroom rather than posted on a digital class website. More people can see them, and they can't get passed around on social media. You know what will work best for your students. Let them personalize the display with their own touches. Invite them to add their own drawings. Figure 16.2 shows a family board that Serena used in her classroom.

Photos show students at the school football game, doing skateboarding tricks, or even just sitting in front of the school. Family boards show students that you honor who they are as human beings. They also help students feel like they belong to your classroom. These are all time management wins.

There is only one of you and many of your students. We love them all, but rarely is there enough time in the day, the week, or even the school year to foster a connection with every student every day. Our students need to be seen and heard and to feel valued. When we take steps to connect with students in more creative ways, we save ourselves time in the long run with fewer behavior issues, a more positive classroom culture, increased learning in the classroom, and happier students. Happier students means happier teachers.

**Figure 16.2**   Family Board

## Your Turn

1.  What additional strategies would you add to our list of eight?

2.  Pick one of these strategies and jot down ideas for how you would enhance it.

3.  Which of these eight suggestions will you start using immediately? Why?

## STRATEGY #17

# Peer Mediators to Save Time in Your Classroom

*Peer mediation is a chance for students to work with other students to help them resolve problems, arguments, disagreements without having to get the teacher or the administration involved.*

—Janet Reno, former U.S. attorney general

Let's get real for a second: How much time per week would you say you find yourself resolving minor conflicts between students? And are these conflicts something you need to be involved in?

We can help. According to a study conducted by Child Trends,

there are five critical skills most likely to increase the odds of success across all outcomes, and which employers expect employees to have: social skills, communication skills, and higher-order thinking skills (including problem solving, critical thinking, and decision making); supported by the intrapersonal skills of self-control and positive self-concept. (Lippman, Ryberg, Carney, & Moore, 2015)

Peer mediation helps students learn all of these skills. It will dramatically help with time management in the classroom because you will no longer have to waste time asking Consuelo to give Aria her pencil back or telling Jayquan to apologize to Roberto for accidentally bumping his chair. To be on the same page, we want you to know that the most fundamental benefits of peer mediation are described below:

- Effectively resolves student conflicts

- Enables students to develop lifelong conflict resolution skills

- Encourages students to accept responsibility for their actions

- Empowers students

- Increases self esteem

- Is preventive and helps students develop their moral framework during the years they attend school

- Builds empathy

- Gives students a voice

- Gives students a safe space

- Shows your students that you trust them

- Improves your classroom climate

- *Saves you time*

Peer mediation is relatively new. It's done in a variety of different ways. The format we advocate here has been shown to benefit more students simultaneously. It will reduce the amount of time you spend intervening in minor conflicts, especially as the year goes on and students get better and more skilled at mediating their own issues. With peer mediation, students work out their own problems, freeing you up to focus on student learning.

Most schools that use peer mediators train a group of responsible students to help other students resolve their issues. What if we shifted our thinking and trained all of them? Training all of your students provides them with essential skills and saves you the time of having to wait for a designated peer mediator to show up in your classroom.

Tamra Nast, a former elementary school teacher, shares how she used peer mediation in her fifth-grade classroom.

Based upon research on conflict resolution and peer mediation skills and programs, I created the "Solve-It-Spot." Our school made the decision to train all students in conflict resolution skills and then have students each choose their personal peer mediator as situations occurred. We asked them to choose someone of good character who would be honest so the situation could get resolved, not necessarily the student's best friend. The students lived up to our expectations and were very thoughtful in choosing the person who would be able to help them in each situation. Interestingly, it was not always the same person.

We trained all students during the first month of each school year. We designed our peer mediation program to align with our social, emotional, and character development standards. When we first began, teachers were very skeptical about spending time out of their teaching day to do this training. However, we discovered that teachers were able to save time in the long run. The smaller conflicts were resolved through students going to the "Solve-It-Spot" in the classroom or on the playground, and the teachers only needed to step in for serious situations. Because of its success, the "Solve-It-Spot" moved to other elementary schools within the district.

Here are the guidelines we used:

Step 1: Look at the other person. (Eye contact and active listening) (Standing or sitting in the spot)

Step 2: Tell them calmly what happened and how you feel about it. (Using just facts and "I" statements)

Step 3: Tell what *you* did to keep the problem going.

Step 4: State what you will do so this doesn't happen again.

Step 5: Each person involved completes a reflection sheet and submits it so that the teacher has a record of the solution reached by the students.

We also used laminated spots or hula hoops so the students could stand or sit in them to calm down. We had spots painted on our playground for recess. Students could choose a peer mediator to join them if they needed a third person to mediate. The program really helped in offering students constructive choices for resolving their conflicts.

Peer mediation offers students real tools that they will use throughout their lives to be successful in interpersonal interactions. Students have shared with us that they use these skills when conflicts arise with their family and friends.

Peer mediation should be used to address minor peer-to-peer issues to prevent tensions escalating into larger issues. It will prevent time and energy-draining situations like this:

[Ed] It's a Friday in mid-June—hot and humid—the last fifty-minute period of the day. The students and I sit in an unair-conditioned classroom on the second floor, windows wide open. I have thirty-one students, and twenty are boys (my penalty for being the assistant principal in charge of discipline). I follow my lesson plan—review the week's civics content and discussion followed by the end-of-the-week quiz.

As I pass out the quiz, Jimmy jumps out of his seat (front row, left side) announcing, "Mr. D, you're an SOB!" (He, however, uses the actual words.)

I respond, "Jimmy! Sit down! Your know nothing about my heritage."

Butch, Jimmy's best friend (front row, right side—same reason why Jimmy's up front, left side) shouts, "Hey, Mr. D, what's a heritage?"

I silently pray (don't let people tell you that teachers in public schools don't pray), *Dear God, please ring the dismissal bell.*

In our experience, classrooms that have a strong peer mediation program in place would never reach this point because students who feel empowered don't tend to lash out at the teacher in this manner. Students who know that you care about them will treat you with respect. Classrooms where students feel safe, cared for, and empowered tend to be much calmer, less disruptive spaces where learning can thrive.

## Your Turn

1. How much time do you spend in your classroom mediating little disagreements between students? Do these mediations usually end well?

2. If you began peer mediation training at the beginning of each school year, do you believe all of your students could be trained as peer mediators? Why or why not?

3. How does peer mediation help you save time while also empowering your students?

4. Would peer mediation also help with your classroom climate and your overall well-being as a teacher?

# PART III

## AT SCHOOL

*It was my last class of the day and I was teaching my students mindfulness and how to relax so they wouldn't be stressed during testing. One of my girls fell asleep. We couldn't wake her up. I ended up just leaving her and kept going with my lesson. It took her friends about ten minutes to get her to wake up to go home.*

*—Celina, middle school science teacher in California*

# STRATEGY #18

# Healthy Habits
# With Curriculum

. . . . . . . . . . . . . . . . . . . . . . . . . . . . . . . . . . . . . . . . . . . . . . . . . . .

*The soul, like the body, accepts by practice whatever habit one wishes to contact.*

*—Socrates*

We wanted to dedicate a chapter to curriculum because it is the mothership of time management. The key is to plan ahead, stay consistent, and set a designated time you plan each week. Make that time a priority.

Think of planning for curriculum like planning a workout regimen. It's tough at first. If any of you have tried to form a workout plan, you know that it's most effective to hit the gym at the same hour each day. Some of us are morning people and some are evening people. It's a guarantee that some days we don't feel like exercising. However, if we commit to a specific time, we will be more likely to go out of habit. Even if we go reluctantly, we usually leave the gym feeling better, on track with our physical development, and committed. Have a sacred workout time that you commit to for a month, a few months, or a year. You'll have a better chance of meeting your exercise goal.

Just like with going to the gym, there will always be something that you could do instead of lesson planning. However, for your own work success and the education of your students, there is nothing more important than lesson planning. No parent phone call, no grading, no student conference is more important than lesson planning for the next week or even the next unit. Remember that.

[Serena] One year I had a personal trainer from 9 a.m. to 10 a.m. every Wednesday. I had a fairly flexible work schedule and thought a morning work-out midweek would be a great reenergizer and also help my productivity and mindset at work. The first few times I went it was great! However, as the weeks went on, work picked up and there were many mornings when I wasn't chirpy when I showed up for my training sessions, to put it lightly. I mentally let other things take priority—and there was always something else to do. I even switched a few times to 6 p.m. after work but found myself canceling for various reasons. My trainer and I had a talk and committed to 9 a.m., rain or shine, tired or not, stressed or not, every Wednesday. After a while, it became easier because I subconsciously knew that was my workout day and my work-out time. It became easier to get there every week and the workouts seemed easier to get through.

Committing to a set time for curriculum planning works the same way. If you plan alone, choose a prep period each week (we recommend the same day) that you plan for the next week. Prep periods are more effective for curriculum planning because you know that your other life commitments won't get in the way. If you try to designate Wednesday at 6 p.m. to be your planning time, chances are a dinner or a friend's birthday will pop up, or your distant relative will call during that time. For a better chance of success, pick one prep period per week that is dedicated to curriculum planning. Put it on your calendar and let your mentor teacher, coach, and teacher colleagues know that that is your designated planning day.

[Serena] My co-teachers and I always planned on Thursday during our prep. We knew not to schedule any parent meetings, student meetings, or errands on that day, and we always met in the same place. We closed the door, turned off our phones, and respected the time. Because of this we felt appreciation for each other and were a tight-knit group. We set a goal for each prep period that we would have the objectives, daily lessons, guiding questions, learning activities, and assessments ready for the next week. On Friday we would divide up the material needs and made sure copies, model essays, etc. were done before we left that weekend. If during prep a thought popped into our head that needed discussing, such as Amir's yelling in class or Ben's issue with Tenisha's assignment, we had a stack of sticky notes. We wouldn't bring the issue up vocally; we would grab a sticky and write it down. We saved ten minutes at the end of the meeting to discuss individual student issues. Lesson planning takes priority over individual student issues. It's that simple. It eliminates the need for planning all weekend for the week and running behind on the curriculum-planning treadmill.

Tips for managing your weekly planning meetings to gain desired curriculum results include the following:

▶ Set an agenda each week if you plan with others. If you have to talk about Kyoko's outburst in class, do it, but set a time limit. Talk about what happened, why, and how you will proceed. I suggest three minutes per student. Limit this to ten minutes of your planning period.

▶ Remember the goal is to have the next week's lessons planned so you can divide up the work.

▶ Try using Google Docs. You can all type as you are discussing the lesson so one person isn't doing the bulk of the work.

▶ Be sure to list the materials you will need for the next week in the agenda. My co-teacher used to keep all of these materials in a large box behind our desk. Then we arrived to school on Monday a few minutes early and had everything we needed to set up the classroom for learning that day. It was glorious.

▶ Set ten minutes at the beginning or the end of the meeting to talk about individual student needs and modifications and accommodations needed for students. The trick is to set a time limit on this. We all love our students; we could talk about them all day. However, the planning must remain the focus of this meeting.

▶ Put a sticky note next to your computer or notebook as you plan. If something comes up that you'd like to discuss, save it for the designated ten minutes at the end of the meeting. The curriculum must take the forefront of these meetings.

When it comes to curriculum, it's not about finding time to plan, it's about dedicating a consistent time to planning each week and sticking to it. Everything else has to fall to the side during that time.

I'll be real with you: There were times when I didn't feel like I was ready to plan for the next week. I was still dealing with Jonny's angry parents, or Sarah's failing grade. However, similar to the effects that occur when we push ourselves to get to the gym at our sacred time, I left the Thursday planning session every week feeling prepared and mentally clear, and I knew I was putting curriculum at the forefront of my priorities. If you plan at the same time each week, you are more likely to stick to that because it will become a habit. You will no longer be trying to fit in planning; it will be something you just do every week at a certain time.

---

[Serena] As I stated in my first book, *Real Talk About Classroom Management*, "Curriculum and instruction is the mothership of classroom management. If you can plan instruction that is rigorous, engaging, collaborative, and connected to the real world, your behavior problems will start to disappear" (2018, p. 83). When you hold yourself accountable to your planning day, time, and outcomes, this happens. When your behavior issues start to disappear, you have more time and energy to work on productive tasks for your school, classroom, and students. Our students need us to be committed and form healthy habits regarding when we plan, how we plan, and what we accomplish during our planning meetings.

## Your Turn

1. Do you think this proposed curriculum-making plan is possible for you? If it is not, what do you need to do to make it possible? What is getting in the way of your setting aside a dedicated time for curriculum planning? What can you do about overcoming that obstacle?

2. What is your current curriculum-making "workout schedule?" What day/time during the week do you devote to planning? If you don't have a set time, you can choose one now. If you have a co-teacher it should optimally be set with him or her.

3. How would you feel if you could leave work every Friday with the next week's lessons and materials already prepared?

# STRATEGY #19

# Groupwork

. . . . . . . . . . . . . . . . . . . . . . . . . . . . . . . . . . . . . . . . . . . . . . . . . . . . . . . . . . . . .

*Never confuse movement with action.*

—*Ernest Hemingway*

Have you ever planned a really great lesson and included groupwork just to make the lesson more exciting for students? Once the students enter the room, you explain the assignment and have them form groups. They fight over who they are going to choose, argue with one another, complain that they don't like their groups, and start moving desks. Ellen accidentally bumps Pam with her chair as she is moving. Three groups are too close to one another, and one group of students is all the way in the corner and already taking out their cell phones as if this were "free time." You think, *Oh no! What have I done?*

[Serena] This used to happen during my second year of teaching. The reason it didn't happen in my first year is that I was too scared to take students out of their rows. It took me a few years and lots of trial by fire to figure out what makes groupwork do just that—work. What usually ended up happening was I would yell and demand students put their desks back in rows, explain they "couldn't handle it," and say they had to do the assignment solo. I was angry, they were angry, and their self-esteem lowered. The air of the classroom grew stiff and toxic. It pains me to remember this all-too-common scenario. Looking back now, I wonder: Why were they able to do the task alone?

For groupwork to be effective, it should only be undertaken with tasks that are complex enough that one group member cannot do it alone. If the task can be completed by one student working alone, then there is no reason to attempt it as a group.

If you want strategies for managing behavior during groupwork, see *Real Talk About Classroom Management*. Here's a refresher:

▶ Consider how you want to group the students.

▶ Arrange group seats before students enter the classroom.

▶ Give each student a role.

▶ Provide both written and verbal instructions.

▶ Use a rubric and a daily point system. (2018, p. 126)

Each of these strategies will help save you valuable time with groupwork. For Strategy #19 in this book, we'll cover how to help students manage their time effectively during groupwork. Below are a couple of tips you can use.

## Tip #1: Ask the Loner

Here is a tip from Strategy #26 in *Real Talk for Classroom Management*:

If you are going to have students choose groups, there's a strategy you can use to make sure everybody feels included. When there's a student whom the others naturally don't choose for their groups, it's usually because of that student's inability to work well in a team. The student rarely can identify this and rewords it as "I like to work alone." It's okay for a student to work alone for some tasks, but students need to know how to work in teams to get a job done. These are 21st-century skills. When I have one of these students in my class, I usually ask her the day before I plan on doing groupwork which student she works well with in the classroom. I'll do this in casual conversation. Chances are she'll name someone you didn't expect. Let's say Amy is the student who is never picked for groups. Amy tells me in conversation that she works well with Darin. Early the next day I'll put a sticky note on Darin's desk asking, "Will you ask Amy to be in your group when I have the class choose groups today?" I'll hold the note there for a few seconds, wait until the student says "yes," and then I'll crumple it up and throw it away so Amy never sees the note. When I announce it's time to choose groups, Darin walks over to Amy and asks her to be in his group. Amy will most likely be sheepish and shy. She'll say "sure" and maybe shrug her shoulders like she doesn't care. Don't look over at this point. Amy will look at you to see if you had anything to do with it. (Pariser, 2018, p. 127)

Although this strategy was originally written for a book on classroom management, I included it here in a book on time management because it will save time. If Amy doesn't work with anybody and the task you assigned is challenging enough that a partner is necessary, Amy is going to need help. Who do you think she will ask if she doesn't feel like she is part of the class? You or another adult in the classroom. That means that one adult is tied to one student and can't help or assist any other students. This is really poor time management as it will result in the other students struggling.

## Tips for Making Groupwork Work

- **Consider how you want to group the students.** There are many ways to group students. Think about the goal you want them to accomplish. Is the assignment harder than what they could do on their own? If so, do heterogeneous grouping. This means that you will have students of different skill levels together. This way, each group has a mini-teacher to help them. If you do not group this way, all the low-level students will sink together. This is a nightmare for everybody. You could also let the students work in pairs, or in groups of three. Groups of four to six are usually the most productive, and the larger size gives them more power to perform.

- **Arrange group seats before students enter the classroom.** Arrange desks and chairs for groupwork before the students walk into the room. A lot of the success of groupwork is a function of how well the desks are arranged. If one desk is pushed out to the side, that student may subconsciously feel as if she is not part of the group. Perhaps even give a group the option of sitting on a carpeted floor in a well-liked or comfy corner of the room. I usually don't force students to sit on the floor. That just seems cruel. (Some girls feel uncomfortable sitting on the floor in skirts, it hurts some larger students' legs, etc.) If you give them the option, one or two groups will usually jump at the opportunity, even in high school.

- **Give each student a role.** Make sure all students are carrying their own weight. For example, one student could be the motivator. Another student could be the recorder. The third student could be the acknowledger to make sure everyone is participating. You can also assign a group leader who reports to you. I've also had groups and didn't assign roles to let the natural strengths surface organically. It's really all about what your tasks are, what age you're working with, and knowing your students.

- **Provide both written and verbal instructions.** Groups will usually fall apart only when they do not know what to do or are not held accountable. Make sure

*(Continued)*

(Continued)

there are written as well as spoken directions to the groups. Desks are usually arranged all around the room with groupwork, so it's a good idea to have a set of written directions or procedures for each group of students.

- **Use a rubric and a daily point system.** If needed, you can give students a participation grade or points each day based on how well they are working in a group. Before they start the groupwork, go over a written rubric showing how they will be graded during groupwork. A rubric with examples will prevent arguments. Be sure to actually go over and teach the rubric before the assignment. If you quickly score the students in class (if a participation grade is based on work produced and behavior), and they see the points immediately and in writing, this is very effective in either maintaining the stellar behavior and work completion for the next day or empowering them to change their behavior the next day in groups.

# Tip #2: Give Each Student a Distinct Role in the Group

In this chapter I want to go deeper into giving each student a role. This keeps time management flowing in a group. Imagine the students are in groups and ready to work. You explain the task, they get started, and then about ten minutes in you look around and notice half of the class has stopped working. Skylar is taking a nap; Sam is checking her phone. Rob is trying to work but he can't get any of his group members to help him so he ends up doing the assignment alone. Ben is staring at the ceiling because he wants to help but Rob doesn't know how to explain things to him. You can tell that Sloane is on the cusp of either checking in or checking out . . . when she isn't telling Skylar how useless she is to the group. Skylar pretends not to hear her.

Well, the good news is that this scenario is much better than a toxic combination of students and argumentative groups, but they still are not learning. Groupwork should be the students working toward a common goal and using each other's strengths, skills, and talents to get there. This means they could be

▶ dividing up a large task so they each do a part to make one large collective product (we see this commonly in projects);

▶ discussing ideas together to push each other's thinking (this one is especially powerful);

▶ helping each other figure out complex problems orally or in writing; or

▶ jigsawing information.

It is important to make sure that students are fully progressing. First, it's important that you check in with each group. One of the beautiful aspects of groupwork is that the teacher rotates to check in on or push the thinking of five to six groups rather than thirty to forty individual students. Managing six groups takes less energy and time from you. *wink*

To keep the pace up in the groups, assign each student a role. Roles are a scaffold for productivity in groupwork. If your students tend to forget their roles, have them wear badges identifying their roles. You can make the role badges different colors so you can identify each role quickly with just a glance. This works best with younger grades. It also saves you time.

The Process Oriented Guided Inquiry Learning Project (2017) suggests these four roles:

1. **Manager or facilitator**: Helps make sure the group stays on task and is focused and that there is room for everyone in the conversation.

2. **Recorder**: Keeps a record of those in the group and the roles that they play in the group. The recorder also records critical points from the small group's discussion along with findings or answers.

3. **Spokesperson or presenter:** Presents the groups ideas to the rest of the class. The spokesperson should rely on the notes from the recorder to present to the class.

4. **Reflector** or **strategy analyst**: Observes team dynamics and guides the consensus-building process (helps group members come to a common conclusion).

The Teaching Center (2019) suggests using the additional three roles below for groups with more than four members:

1. **Encourager**: Encourages group members to continue to think through their approaches and ideas. Middle and elementary school students can cheer each other on. Yes, it's corny, but we know that happier students learn more. The Encourager uses probing questions to help facilitate deeper thinking and group-wide consideration of ideas.

[Serena] I always like to have an encourager. It's such a great role and puts a smile on everybody's face. We know that happy students learn more.

2. **Questioner**: Pushes back when the team comes to a consensus too quickly without considering a number of options or points of view. The questioner makes sure that the group hears varied points of view and is not avoiding potentially rich areas of disagreement.

3. **Checker**: Checks over work in problem-solving contexts before the group members finalize their answers.

If you are working on social skills in your classroom, you could provide sentence stems of words or phrases students can use in each role. This may be necessary for elementary school but not for high school, or perhaps for one period of students but not the other. The class that doesn't seem to need the stems, however, may actually find them helpful to use. You decide what will benefit your students the most.

So how do you assign the roles? I've found it most powerful when the students decide who performs each role. Students who are nominated by their classmates for a particular role often feel empowered. Maybe Skylar's group will dedicate her as the manager and she will have a reason to stay awake and feel empowered because others are relying on her. She will feel like she is adding value to her group instead of napping like she has before.

You also can project a timer on your document camera if possible. Write what task students should have completed after a certain amount of time. This is particularly helpful if groups are competing against one another or supposed to be working at the exact same pace. For example, you might set the timer for twenty minutes and seventeen seconds (I always add in a random amount of seconds just to get a student giggle). Then write "Introduction completed by this time" under the timer on a sticky note.

Please remember, a scaffold should only be implemented if needed. If you have a class that thrives during groupwork and pushes each other's thinking, then giving them this scaffold could actually hinder them. It's like putting training wheels on an Olympic cycler's bike. It would probably make them go slower and they will become frustrated. Our job is to know when our students need the training wheels or extra support and when they don't.

## Your Turn

1. Have you ever assigned students roles in groups? What were the roles? Did they work?

2. Are there any roles in this chapter that you'd like to try assigning?

3. How does groupwork help you have a more efficient and meaningful dialogue and check for understanding logistically with your class?

4. What other skills does groupwork teach students in your classroom?

# STRATEGY #20

# When We Have
# to Be Present

........................................................................

*Mindfulness isn't difficult; we just need to remember to do it.*

—*Sharon Salzberg*

In just one class period you could have phones ringing, students laughing, students asking questions, e-mails flooding in, parents asking questions, fire drills, lesson planning, and grading. We get it. Teaching is a profession where you are constantly around a lot of people. You are going to be around more distractions than someone who sits in a quiet office or cubicle all day. There may be a significant number of distractions, but the good news is you have the ability to control most of them.

There is one time that we have to put all of our distractions aside: during instruction. This is the most important time to us as teachers and the most critical for our students' learning. If we are not present during instruction, we're missing the entire point. When we are our best selves during instruction, everything else starts to fall into place at school. We have fewer discipline problems that take up our time, we can address student questions more accurately, and we become more engaging in our delivery of curriculum. This all leads to fewer reteaching sessions and to more connected students, which leaves us with more time throughout the school day.

In order to be fully present during instruction, we'd like to suggest three mindfulness activities to try before you teach a lesson.

# 1. Take a Brisk Walk

This walk can be around your school grounds or, better yet, on your athletic track so you aren't pulled aside for questions from other teachers or administrators. I've personally seen teachers take walks together around their school track during a planning period. This was at a school that had low turnover and high teacher satisfaction. Administration, if you are reading this, please be happy if you see your teachers doing this, especially if it is before they are teaching students or in between teaching periods. They are preparing themselves to have more mental clarity, increased patience, and presence during lessons. Well done, teachers!

Take a walk without your phone. When you are texting or checking e-mail or social media during your walk, you are clogging your head. The purpose of the walk is to get your thoughts flowing freely, unraveling the jumble. Unplug. What if somebody needs to get ahold of you while you are on the walk? Trust us, they'll be fine for ten to twenty minutes. Your well-being is more important.

# 2. Write It Down

We wish that we could wipe away all of the inherent stresses that come with teaching. In an article on stress in the *Guardian's* "Secret Teacher" series, a secondary school teacher in England wrote, "In one day we not only teach, we manage behavior, plan lessons, assess learning, counsel students, carry out first aid, reply to a long list of emails, write reports, tidy classrooms, create resources, mark books, and create displays—the list is endless" ("Secret Teacher," 2013).

"Write It Down" is a mindfulness strategy that helps you process stress. It will help you strengthen your patience, improve your working memory, and strengthen your mind to keep that love of teaching alive. We need our brains in top condition.

Sometimes there will be something at work or at home that is frustrating you or continually popping into your head so that you can't get it out of your mind. You may feel like your mind is going in circles replaying conversations and doing everything but staying in the present. If there is something upsetting you, annoying you, and/or keeping you from being able to focus, try writing it down. This can be in the notes section of your phone, on a paper tablet you keep in your desk, or in a Word document you keep on your computer desktop. Writing down your frustrations and then listing one to two things you can do about them right now will prevent you from obsessing over the problems in your head. Once you've put an issue down in writing and noted some possible solutions, your mind is then free to focus on something else, such as instruction.

## 3. Meditate

You've all heard of meditation by now. You might have thought, *How the heck do I have time to meditate? That's some hippy stuff.* Meditation doesn't have to take a long time; it can take just two minutes. You can gradually progress up to ten minutes or so over time, but start with two for now. Try it every day before school, after lunch, or during your prep. YouTube has some great guided meditation videos that you can use. According to a 2014 study, transcendental meditation at least once a day has been found to substantially reduce teacher stress, depression, and burnout (Elder, Nidich, Moriarty, & Nidich, 2018). Many people have been fascinated with how much meditation has strengthened their ability to perform at work. This is especially important for teachers. We are asked to make thousands of decisions every day and interact with many children, colleagues, administrators, and parents daily. On top of everything else, we are asked to teach, and teach well. We need our brains in tip-top shape.

A 2018 study gave a group of teachers access to mindfulness programs. The results suggested that mindful-based interventions improved teachers' awareness, cognitive ability, and working memory, and the teachers experienced greater awareness of their physical surroundings. The results also suggested that "the amount of stress teachers experience is less important than how they conceptualize their stress. Teachers who developed resilience exercised mindful awareness and nonreactivity coupled with a healthy distress of tolerance and sense of efficacy" (Donahoo, Siegrist, and Garrett-Wright, 2018). By efficacy, we mean the belief you have in yourself. The thought that "Hey, I got this! I can do this."

A few schools have gone so far as to implement a school-wide meditation program that has the entire school meditate at the same time, sitting comfortably and with eyes closed. These programs have been reported to reduce psychological distress, including anxiety and depression, and promote overall mental and physical health (Maharishi University of Management, 2014). You can start with yourself and your classroom. *Namaste.*

In addition to instruction, another time we need to be fully present is while giving students feedback face to face. This can be in a 1:1 setting or even in a group of a few students. Too often we are tempted to have our phone with us during this time. This communicates to students that they are only important until something *dings* on your phone. When you are giving feedback, having a phone next to you on the desk or somewhere else in sight is the equivalent of having dinner with a friend that you haven't seen for a long time and letting your phone interrupt the conversation. Think about it: How often do we give 1:1 face time feedback to each student? For us, we do it all the time, but that student is one of many. We ask that you give each student the attention they deserve and keep the phone out of sight and silence it if it is in your pocket.

In 2008 John Hattie conducted a synthesis of over 800 meta-analyses relating to student achievement. He found that giving students feedback was a leading factor in improving student achievement (Hattie, 2008). When students get valuable uninterrupted feedback, they will very likely perform better in your class. If students are performing better academically in your class, you will have to spend less time on parent phone calls or on redirecting negative behaviors. This means more time for you.

The other factor that was at the top of improving student achievement was teacher-student relationships. We've already covered this in other chapters, but it appears in Hattie's work as well. Being present during 1:1 feedback will strengthen your relationships with students. You are saying to them, "You are the most important person I could be talking to right now."

## Your Turn

1. How do you feel when you are teaching? Do you feel present? If not, what is one thing you could change to help you feel more present?

2. Out of the three strategies listed to help you "be present," which appeals more to you and why?

3. Is there someone at school who could be your accountability partner for a "staying present" activity you'd like to try? Who is that person?

# STRATEGY #21

# Manage Time
# in Your Lessons

*To achieve great things, two things are needed; a plan, and not quite enough time.*

—*Leonard Bernstein*

[Serena] I once knew a teacher who often complained that her lessons would drag on forever. For this story's sake, we'll call her Ms. Longlesson. Ms. Longlesson would often say things like, "We barely got through the first five minutes of my lesson! It took forty-five minutes for the warm up! I was disciplining the entire time and we couldn't get through anything." This set off huge red flags in my head.

A powerful lesson plan consists of content that is challenging to students, offers support to help them access the information, and engages them. It should also have a sense of urgency.

▶ When we create lesson plans, there should be times next to each activity indicating how long it should take. Using a timer is very helpful for staying on schedule. Make the timer visible to the students as well. This can add a sense of urgency and make sure the students keep up the pace.

Students will often take as long as you let them. Or, let's be real, they will rush through an activity and then sit without anything to do. Make an effort to maintain a healthy pace to keep everybody in a similar stride of productive work.

▶ Mention the timer in your lesson dialogue. Say something like, "Okay, you'll have three minutes and ten seconds (just to add some fun and keep them on their toes) to complete this problem." This way, the students who work too quickly know they have an entire three minutes, and the students who work too slowly know they only have three minutes. Then, make the timer visible to students and monitor their progress. They will pace themselves. You can even empower the students by asking one to set the timer.

▶ If you have another adult or a co-teacher in your classroom, have them keep time during certain parts of the lesson. My co-teacher and I used to do this. When I had two minutes left to finish the warm-up, she would signal this to me by holding up two fingers. When she led the lesson, I would do the same for her. Often, I would ask so the class could hear, "How much time do I have left?" This way the students knew we were on a schedule and there wasn't a minute to waste.

Figure 21.1, drawn from *Real Talk About Classroom Management* (Pariser, 2018), presents an example of how much time you should commit to each part of a lesson in middle school. Adjust as necessary for elementary, high school, or adult learners.

Doing this not only keeps track of time spent on the different parts of your lesson but also models time management skills for your students. *Real Talk About Classroom Management* goes into more detail about managing time in lessons with different grades (Pariser, 2018).

**Figure 21.1**   Example of Chunking and Planning Pace in a Lesson

| Minutes | Lesson Objective: |
|---|---|
| | Given a collection of poems, students will analyze personification by explaining and illustrating personification in poems on graphic organizer. |
| 5 | Anticipatory Set: Watch the short two-minute clips from *Beauty and the Beast* that include many examples of personification. Ask students to jot down responses: What did you notice the objects doing in the movie that they can't do in real life? Example answers: dancing teacups, laughing water |
| | Share responses with neighbor, then class. |
| 5 | Model: Project a model poem with personification using a document camera. Show explanations and illustrations already completed next to specific lines in poem (to save time) about why it is personification (using metacognition) as students watch you think aloud. |
| | As a class, construct a class definition for personification and compare with a definition that can be found online. |
| 10 | Guided: After reading a second poem with the class at their seats, have students repeat lines after you using the SDAIE (specifically designed academic instruction in English) strategy Choral Response. Then have table groups of students work together to explain which lines of the poem contain personification and why in writing (just as you did for the model poem). Next, have individual students quickly sketch pictures illustrating personification in the second poem, as well as compose a mini-paragraph about personification in it (to up the rigor, since they have been working with table groups). |
| 10 | Independent: Have individual students start to work independently to complete a graphic organizer to analyze a third poem with the same explanations and illustrations as they did for the first two poems. They can finish the paragraph for this poem for homework if needed. |
| 5 | Closure: Ask students to write down three other examples of personification on an exit slip to assess understanding of your teaching. Have students talk with a partner and share their learning with the class. |

*Source:* Pariser, 2018.

## Your Turn

1. How would using a timer while teaching help you in your classroom?

2. What are other ideas you have about how to manage time during your lessons?

3. Have you ever tried teaching with a timer? Did you feel it helped the pacing of the lesson? If yes, why do you think this is the case?

# STRATEGY #22

# Technology

*A worksheet is still a worksheet whether it's on a computer or on a sheet of paper you pass out. Sometimes it's faster just to pass out the piece of paper.*

—Laura K. Spencer, president of San Diego CUE

[Serena] Computers aren't smarter than people—they are just faster. They do not think critically, they are not creative, and they don't solve problems. This concept was repeated over and over during my studies at San Diego State University for a master's in educational technology. Furthermore, a computer should never be used as a behavior management tool or as a fancy typewriter. I'll be the first to admit that it is very tempting to use computers in this way, especially when we are tired. There is currently a big push for 1:1 laptops in schools, especially in low-income schools, which is wonderful. But there can be a downside to the overuse or misuse of computers. We all know that colleague that overuses 1:1 laptops as a digital behavior management tool. Let's not do that.

Based on his synthesis of 1,600 meta-analyses involving 300 million students, John Hattie (2018) concluded that a laptop for every student is only "likely to have a small positive impact on student achievement." In fact, mobile phones were rated to have a higher impact on student achievement than 1:1 laptops (Hattie, 2018). We should use technology in the classroom, but it should not replace paper. We should use it to accentuate learning and to break down the four walls of a classroom. Consider the following four points for managing time.

# 1. Sometimes a Pen and Paper Is Faster

This is true for both you and your students. Before you implement technology, think to yourself, *Is it more efficient and does it result in just as usable of a product to use pen and paper?* For example, an exit slip that just you will read or a quick jot activity that just one person needs to read can be completed faster when using pen and paper than if you tried to use a computer. Also, pens and papers don't crash. However, the downfall is that it's difficult logistically to see everybody else's responses with pen and paper.

# 2. Sometimes Technology Enhances Collaboration

If you want to increase collaboration or have the class to be able to read everybody's responses, pen and paper can be less than effective. You could have the students write a quick jot that gets posted on a digital community board so the class can see everyone's contributions at once. The benefit of using technology for this is that the class can use the responses to engage in rich conversation. There is also far less wasted paper, and the answers can be kept to reference later. Also, students can keep contributing to the conversation at home, so the learning doesn't have to stop when the bell rings.

# 3. Have a Backup Plan if Your Lesson Relies Solely on Technology

There's this unwritten rule that we don't find out about until we get our own classrooms: If we set up a lesson that is solely reliant on technology, we will forget to charge our computer cart the night before, or the WiFi in our classroom will go out. Always have a backup plan so the students are not wasting valuable learning time while you are trying to work with your technology department to get your WiFi started.

Laura Spencer, San Diego CUE president, presented to educational leaders at the 2019 California Teachers Performance Assessment conference as the keynote speaker. She suggested three questions to ask yourself when deciding if and when to implement technology in your lesson:

1. Is it the same level of learning if it is done with pencil and paper?

2. Does technology use break down the four walls of the classroom for this lesson?

3. Does using technology in this lesson help provide an authentic audience? (Note: In education, we use the term *authentic audience* when the students have a chance to share their learning with somebody besides the teacher and their classmates. In other words, does technology help connect students with an audience, either virtually or face to face, that is relevant to the material but different from, or in addition to, the teacher or students in the class? An example of an authentic audience could be politicians from the community if the students are doing a project on climate change.)

## 4. Try Blended Learning

Technology is best used in partnership with you as the teacher. Think of it as your co-teacher, not your replacement. Use tech to help your class function more effectively. Catlin Tucker (2013) defined blended learning as "combin[ing] classroom learning with online learning, in which students can, in part, control the time, pace, and place of their learning." She also wrote, "I advocate a teacher-designed blended learning model, in which teachers determine the combination that's right for them and their students" (Tucker, 2013). Simply put, this means that a portion of the time the students are listening to you and a portion of the time they are learning from a computer. How does this help with time management? Here are four ways:

1. Fewer papers to copy, staple, and prepare. Uploading one document for all students to access is much quicker than making 115 copies, not to mention way better for the environment.

2. Less organizational maintenance and fewer stacks of papers. More electronic materials means fewer folders to file, papers to collect, and pencils to sharpen.

3. If your students are engaged with the technology and therefore more eager to participate in the lesson, then you will have fewer behavior management issues.

4. You'll most likely have more energy. Human beings need energy to redirect, motivate, inspire, challenge, and teach. The computer is doing a portion of the work for us in this department. In a sense, you are multiplying yourself around the classroom and personalizing instruction for students without exerting energy having to be everywhere at once.

Here are a few apps for simultaneously enhancing learning *and* saving time:

▶ Menti.com (formative assessments)—for activating prior knowledge, formative assessments, and collaboration

▶ Padlet

▶ Pear Deck

▶ Slido

▶ Book Creator—allows students to create books where the world is their audience (authentic audience)

▶ Underlined—can publish stories for authentic audiences and writing competitions

▶ Word Clouds

▶ Chat rooms where students can participate in book clubs

▶ Pollit

▶ Poll Everywhere

▶ Thin Slides—teaches presentation skills

▶ Wolfram|Alpha—a computational knowledge engine or answer engine to help students with math problems

▶ Adobe Spark—user-friendly website design app for students to showcase knowledge

▶ Apple Clips—Students can demonstrate their knowledge by creating one-to two-minute short clips that are automatically closed-captioned. It is a powerful tool for EL students because they can see video and audio converted into text.

▶ Google Hangouts

▶ Flipgrid

▶ Seesaw

It is important to note that when using technology students should always have an element of collaboration. We have to remember that employers are looking for strong communicators and collaborators. If a student is working on an individual project, at some point in the class there should be a point where they are asked to stop, show a partner something they have created, or talk to a partner about an idea they would like to bounce off of someone. This can be a stopping point you have with the full class or stops can be at staggered times. Schedule a time where you ask students to stop and collaborate, no matter where they are in the project. Sometimes we have to peel students away from computers to do this, but it is necessary because collaboration is so important.

## Your Turn

1. Have you tried blended learning? If you are unsure of what this is, look at the work of Catlin Tucker, Jayme Linton, Kathleen P. Fulton, or Barbara Bray and Kathleen McClaskey.

2. How have you seen technology help with your time management or execution of lessons?

3. How can you ensure you always have a backup plan if (when) technology fails to make sure that learning time is not wasted?

## STRATEGY #23

# Necessary Multitasking

. . . . . . . . . . . . . . . . . . . . . . . . . . . . . . . . . . . . . . . . . . . . . . . . . . . . . . . . . .

*I never multitask.*

*—No teacher ever*

Our experience in the classroom and in life shows that although we shouldn't, we probably multitask during much of the day. In Strategy #15 we reviewed the research on the detrimental effects of multitasking. However, the reality of teaching is that sometimes (oftentimes) multitasking is necessary and unavoidable.

Teachers are expected to (simultaneously) be role models, administrators, disciplinarians, evaluators, facilitators, and sometimes even figurative foster parents. All of these roles must be fulfilled at the same time you are teaching subject matter, adapting the curriculum to meet the needs of your students, preparing students for state and district tests, teaching character education and social and emotional skills, and managing your classroom. It is overwhelming just to write down this list of expectations. But we do these things daily and, for the most part, are very successful at it and well aware that multitasking takes planning, patience, and persistence.

According to an infographic created by TeachThought (2019), "A teacher makes 1,500 decisions a day." That's more than brain surgeons (Boogren, 2016). Outstanding teachers are masters at multitasking. If you have to multitask, do it with care and intention. Here is some advice adapted from wikihow.com/Multitask:

- Establish your main goals for the day. For a prep period, we recommend focusing on three or four achievable goals. You only have limited time.

- For an intense task such as lesson planning for the week, set aside a time you will give it your full focus. Set a timer for, for example, thirty minutes. For less mentally intense tasks, such as making copies or cleaning your whiteboard, it's okay to multitask a bit.

- New tasks may require your full focus. For familiar tasks, you may be okay multitasking.

- If you need to do two things, don't do them at the same time but alternate back and forth. Jugglers do this, as they are focusing on one ball in the air at a time although they have many balls in the air.

- Simplify tasks you can't eliminate.

    1. Complete a bulletin board in fifteen minutes rather than three hours. Who cares if every puffy cloud isn't pinned up perfectly?

    2. Instead of changing out the bulletin board a few times a year, delegate the task to a student or parent.

    3. You could also pick a solid dark color for your bulletin board that will last the entire year.

    4. Seasons and holidays will still come and go even if your bulletin board doesn't reflect this.

    5. Simplifying tasks will conserve your energy and mental space. Parents and students will appreciate this in the long run.

- Keep a list of smaller tasks that could be considered filler tasks on the side of your desk somewhere, but always prioritize your larger ones. Give the larger tasks the bulk of your time.

- Take breaks when needed.

- Don't try to do everything at once. Multitasking on two tasks is different from trying to juggle ten tasks at once. Pick and choose your battles.

- Shut out distractions. Turn off your phone (if possible), put in earphones, etc.

▶ Have sticky notes on hand. If something comes up that is not related to the task you are working on, write it down, put it to the side for later, and focus on what you are doing.

▶ Get in the right frame of mind. Meditate or take a quick walk before you start an important task.

▶ Stay hydrated. Your mind will be clearer and it will help you more in the long run than chugging coffee.

---

[Serena] I have to work not to multitask. Actually, when I was writing this book I was moving apartments at the same time. It was challenging to shut myself off from the world. I had to jot down distractions to revisit later as they floated into my head and try to plow through the task at hand without getting sidetracked. The brain doesn't really want to multitask, and it doesn't perform at optimal levels when we do.

# Your Turn

1. List five strategies you use while multitasking.

2. What tasks do you have during which you absolutely cannot multitask—tasks that require your full attention?

3. Is there a way you can minimize multitasking in your workday? How?

# STRATEGY #24

# Helping Your Students Manage Their Time

........................................................

*Education begins the moment we start seeing children as wise and capable beings. Only then can we play along in their world.*

*—Vincent Gowmon*

Time management isn't a skill that is usually taught in schools, but we shouldn't assume that students come to us with this ability. Just like you, students are being asked to do more today than yesterday. Most likely they are being asked to do more than we did as students. As teachers we often find ourselves becoming frustrated or annoyed when assignments aren't turned in on time or students forget to return permission slips. Ed and I challenge you to flip the script. What if you took a few moments to teach time management just as you would a new concept in your classroom? Teaching time management skills will be most effective if you teach them at the beginning of your school year and revisit the topic often.

The benefits of this approach include the following:

▶ Students will submit their work on time—think of how much time this will save you!

▶ Students will become empowered and feel confident.

- You will not have to waste time following up on late work or placing calls to students' homes.

- Students with good time management skills will enjoy a better quality of life. Teaching these skills is especially important in high-poverty areas where children may not have role models with strong time management skills.

- Time management skills will greatly enhance the learning of students with IEPs. Time management and organizational skills may even be *in* their IEPs, so it's a win-win.

- Teaching time management skills will help alleviate student anxiety, depression, stress, and/or feelings of being overwhelmed. Lessening their stress load means that students will learn more.

- When you teach time management, students will know that you care about them as human beings. This will help foster a strong connection with your students.

There isn't a student out there who wouldn't want to learn how to better manage their time, so engagement would be high during the lesson. Even if students choose not to use the skills, they will still have them in their back pocket. You could also bring parents on board with what you are teaching so they can help support the student by practicing time management at home.

Before we share some specific strategies for helping your students manage their time, we suggest starting with some motivational quotes to get student buy-in. Here are a few, but you can easily find other quotes online as well.

Readiness is the mother of luck.
—Baltasar Gracian

Passion fuels dreams. Commitment fuels action. Get clear about what you want to do and why you want to do it. Take action. Your time is now.
—Julie Connor

> Don't let what you cannot do interfere with what you can do.
> —John Wooden

> Learn how to see. Realize that everything connects to everything else.
> —Leonardo da Vinci

> To accomplish great things, we must not only act, but also dream; not only plan, but also believe.
> —Anatole France

And now, here are some suggestions on how to teach students time management:

▶ Teach students how to make to-do lists. Help them prioritize their activities and workload at home and at school.

▶ Teach students how to use a self-monitoring journal to record how they are using their class time effectively.

▶ Have students partner up and have accountability buddies or gather in groups of three where they check in with each other regularly to see how they are keeping up and organizing their responsibilities. They could also use this time to share time management ideas.

▶ Teach students the difference between busy and productive (see Strategy #3) and how not to spend too much time on one task (show them the car windshield video from Strategy #6). Spending too much time on a nonessential task is a common pitfall for students. They may spend hours looking for a quote to start a paper or countless minutes looking for the perfect picture or image to put on their report cover.

▶ Show students a few apps that can help them manage their time. Here we are some we suggest:

1. Google Calendar

2. Timely

3. Workflow

4. Remember the Milk

5. Evernote

6. MyLifeOrganized

7. Google Keep

As teachers, it's also our responsibility to instill confidence in students as they show progress with time management. Just as we praise students for learning a new concept, we can praise students for demonstrating growth with time management skills. Students can be praised when they

▌ meet deadlines;

▌ finish in-school assignments;

▌ complete tasks; and

▌ remember upcoming meetings and show up early or on time without reminders.

Who doesn't want a classroom where more work is turned in on time, students are more empowered and happier, and students are reminding each other when assignments are due? It's a win-win.

# Your Turn

1. When did you learn time management skills? Who taught you?

2. How will teaching students time management help *your* time management and sanity in your classroom?

3. How would you feel about a teacher who showed you how to manage your time?

# STRATEGY #25

# Get a Handle on Paperwork

*We couldn't find a funny or inspirational quote about paperwork.*

*—Ed and Serena*

When we say get a handle on paperwork, we mean the papers that come from the office and sit in your mailbox, not the ones you grade. That's covered in Strategy #11.

---

[Serena] We're talking about the papers that live on your desk in a pile that seems to grow by the minute. Below is a daily conversation from my first few years of teaching.

Colleague:  "Ms. Pariser, did you see the form I left in your box?"

Me:  "Which form? Was it light blue?"

Colleague:  "The one for Joseph. His IEP meeting is today at 1 p.m."

Me:  "So sorry to have you wait! I'll do it as soon as I get to class."

It got the point where the colleague would follow me to my room and even wait by the door if the form was urgent enough. She knew she had a better

---

chance of getting it if she was in my sight. On some days that particular year, I wished there was a witness protection program for teachers so I could change my appearance and my name, just to be able to run to the office or restroom without getting another request for another form I hadn't yet filled out. I was so overwhelmed with teaching that I was avoiding all of those meaningless and time-wasting forms.

Well, they aren't so meaningless. As fun as they are not, forms—some of them, at least—are what make the school and our classrooms function.

If you've avoided these forms, you end up scrambling to fill them out as your students are filing into class and before you have taken attendance. You start class stressed and not your optimal self.

There is always something that seems more urgent than paperwork. If we are not strong time managers, we become reactive and the squeakiest wheels get the grease. And, well . . . papers don't talk. But putting off paperwork will always come back to haunt us. Also, if our colleagues or administrators have to ask us more than once to complete a form, it can be a waste of valuable time. It can also cause frustration or tension between colleagues. A messy pile of unattended papers on our desk gives us a feeling of being overwhelmed. This is not want we want.

More importantly, that pile sitting on your desk is most likely holding up the operations of your school in some way. Teachers are part of an organization. To run properly, your organization needs your help in filling out the forms.

[Serena] Around year five, colleagues around the school used to thank me for getting my forms in on time. This helped my students who had IEP meetings, improved cohesion within my grade-level team, and made the people I worked closely with felt respected. When I was up to date with my forms, I felt in control. Instead of ducking behind every pole trying to make it to the restroom I was getting smiles and thank-you's in the hallway from colleagues. They felt respected, I was happier, and I was helping the school function better.

So what changes did I make in the above scenario to get on top of paperwork? Here are some tips:

▶ If there is a form you can do right in the mailroom, do it there. Do not even take it back to your room. That means you should take a pen with you when you check your mail.

▶ Set a timer a few times a week. This is a set time you will do paperwork. If you are interrupted, stop the timer. Restart the timer when you start again. Keep doing this until you hit your goal time. Ten minutes is a good amount of time to start.

▶ Keep this mantra in your head: Paperwork makes the school move forward. I know it's corny, but it's true. You can add a jingle to it if you want.

▶ If you run into a roadblock where one particular form is causing you frustration, put it aside and complete another that can be done quickly.

A good practice to maintain is to complete and return any form within seventy-two hours. If it is from administration, you will want to turn it in within forty-eight hours.

## Your Turn

1.  Where does your pile of paperwork live in your classroom? Do you feel like you have control of the pile?

2.  When can you set aside an allotted amount of time in your weekly schedule to complete paperwork? Can you schedule it into your calendar?

3.  What other strategies do you use to get a handle on your paperwork?

# Manage Time in Parent Conferences/ Parent Meetings

*Parent involvement in education is crucial. No matter their income or background, students with involved parents are more likely to have higher grades and test scores, attend school regularly, have better social skills, show improved behavior, and adapt well to school.*

—Responsive Classroom

[Ed] Early on during my fifth-grade year, my father and mother insisted that I go with them to a parent-teacher conference. I knew this was a big deal. We waited in the hallway with other parents giving me that "Why is he here?" stare. I had the same question. I expected to be heckled all the next day by my classmates. Suddenly the classroom door flung open and there stood Ms. Hood. For the first time that I could remember, she was smiling. As far as I knew, she was a grouch. Maybe that was a daytime thing, I thought.

Ms. Hood sat me next to her, both of us facing my parents. She had five cue cards on her desk with a message printed on each in bold letters. Maybe it was a new teacher thing. She started with card one: **Smile and be pleasant.** She glanced up at my parents for a short time. Then she gazed at cue card two: **Stress student's strengths.** That didn't take long, but she did take some time to discuss my strengths. Then all of a sudden things changed—the smile was gone. The third card read: **Be frank about weakness.** Ms. Hood's description of my weaknesses took a while, but we did get to the next topic on cue card four: **Discuss student's social skills, if any.** It seemed like we had been in the room for an hour (although it was actually only about twenty minutes), but finally Ms. Hood looked at the final card: **End the conference on a pleasant note.** This had to be hard for her given the report on my "talents"—or lack thereof.

We're hoping you don't need cue cards like Ms. Hood. However, having a quick five-step plan for parent conferences can save you time and keep you on track. I would alter Ms. Hood's steps somewhat to focus more on the positive, however (see the list that follows). You want the student to leave the discussion feeling empowered about following a plan of action that will help him or her succeed in the classroom. These five simple steps can keep your parent conferences on track:

1. Smile

2. Stress student's strengths

3. Discuss areas of growth

4. Discuss student's social skills (if needed)

5. Co-create a plan of action based on conference discussion. We suggest you jot down the plan of action on a sticky or in an e-mail that is then sent to the parents and the student. The plan of action should be co-created by you, the student, and the parents or guardians.

Sample Plan of Action:

▶ Check in with teacher every Monday before class

▶ Volunteer for lunch duty with younger students on playground

▶ Ask older brother for help with math if/when needed at home

If you follow simple steps to lead and manage time during parent conferences, you can ensure that you stay on task and that meetings last only twenty minutes or less. An efficient twenty-minute meeting can be just as, if not more, powerful than an hour-long conversation. In our many years as teachers, we have participated in many different types of meetings with parents. We want to share a few things that we have learned that may be of help to you.

# 1. Nurture the Whole Child in Partnership With Parents

You are in the relationship business. Both you and the parent are teaching the whole child. You need to know how your students are doing at home. Likewise, parents need to know what's going on in school and particularly in your classroom. They will definitely inquire about their child's academic successes, or lack thereof. Parents will want to know your concerns as well as what you are going to do about those concerns and what they should also be doing to address them. They need information about their child's behavior at school. They need to know about their child's social skills and interactions with their classmates. Most parents believe that their kids are above average, but only half really are!

# 2. Communicate Regularly and Frequently

Communication with parents is essential. Communicate regularly and frequently with your students' parents using methods such as phone calls, e-mail, and social media. Keep families informed about class projects, homework and other assignments, students' accomplishments, and any problems or concerns that may arise.

Be ready to work with parents for the betterment of their child academically, emotionally, and socially. We suggest you carry out a parent survey at the beginning of the year asking parents' preferred method of communication. Jennifer Zimmermaker, a special education teacher, includes the survey on the facing page in her beginning-of-the-year parent letter.

# 3. Be Prepared and Proactive

▶ Know your district and school policies regarding progress reports/report cards and grading. Have this information ready at the meeting.

▶ Send parents informative invitations that include conference dates and times and remind parents that they'll be able to ask questions. This is key because an effective parent-teacher conference is a two-way conversation about a student.

▶ Prepare materials well before the conference. This will help you feel more at ease when families show up at your classroom door. Review student data, assignments, and assessments that you'll be sharing with parents and make notes about what you'd like to ask parents about their children to support learning.

---

Parent communication is essential for a successful school year and is very important to me!

1. How would you prefer to communicate with me? (circle one or more)

   Phone                    E-mail                    Notes Home

2. Please list phone number(s) or e-mail you prefer I use to contact you.

   Guardian #1

       Cell _____

       Home _____

       Work _____

       E-mail _____

   Guardian #2

       Cell _____

       Home _____

       Work _____

       E-mail _____

Sign here to give permission to contact you:

    Guardian #1 Signature _____

    Guardian #2 Signature _____

---

▶ Create a welcoming environment. Make your classroom inviting by displaying students' work, pictures of students doing activities, and so forth. Try not to sit behind your desk; sit at a table with parents. Have paper and pens available so parents can take notes. Have bottles of water available.

# 4. Open With Positives

Discuss progress and growth. Share grade-level expectations and explain how their child is meeting those expectations. Discuss behavior and social skills as well as strengths and needs in each area. Ask questions—what do the parents see to be their child's strengths, weaknesses, needs, interest, and so on. Always let students know you believe in them at the end and that you are excited about the next steps in their scholastic journey.

## 5. Create a Follow-Up Plan

When it is time to end the meeting, ask the parents what they see as the follow-up to the conference. Be prepared to make some suggestions to help them help their child and to identify ways to continue the conversation. Ask, "What is the best way for me to keep in touch with you about (student's) progress?"

Some teachers we know send a thank-you note about one week after the conference. You might have students write thank-you notes to their parents or guardians for attending and supporting their learning. In the note, remind parents to contact you (include your contact information) if they have any further questions or concerns.

Be sure to contact parents who did not attend and offer alternative ways to communicate about their child's progress.

Remember, parents are trying their hardest to do their best for their children. They love their children. They watched them take their first steps and say their first words. They want you to like their children. If you view a child as a failure, the parents see it as indicating that they, too, have failed. Approach the meeting with the attitude of "Let's work together to find a solution" rather than "Look at what Analise did again today."

# Communicating With Parents Who Speak a Different Language Than You

[Serena] Our class was holding a car wash to raise money for a broken computer, and I wanted to enlist parents to help spread the word. I worked in a Latinx neighborhood in San Diego in a Title 1 school that was 98 percent non-white. The only languages I spoke were English and bit of French (which didn't help me much), but I had just discovered a language translation application so I thought I was all set. I made a flyer, then with one click of a mouse—voila!—the flyer was translated into Spanish perfectly . . . or so I thought. I proudly handed out the flyers to students. Quite impressed with myself, I asked the class to flip them over to the Spanish translation on the other side that suggested they could invite their parents if they wished. The class grew silent as they read what I had written. One student started to chuckle. Brows crinkled, and one student looked up at me and said, "Huh?" They started to read it aloud in Spanish, and one girl (one of my biggest behavioral problems) started laughing so hard I thought she was going to fall out of her seat. "We're washing trains, Ms. Pariser? Where? What's a train wash?"

> I'm not sure how the translation application turned *car wash* into *train wash*, but when translation apps were first introduced, they were often less than accurate. Translation applications are much more reliable today. You might be able to speak to a parent using a translation application, but it may frustrate them when you can't understand their responses back to you.

You can't solely rely on translation apps to communicate effectively with speakers of other languages, but luckily my efforts did make the parents feel included and they appreciated the invitation to participate. Remember that parents who speak other languages want to communicate with you. A language barrier should not stop you from doing this.

# Strategies for Overcoming Language Barriers

▶ Celebrate home languages.

Communicate to students that you value the fact that they grew up speaking a different language and learning a culture distinct from mainstream American culture. Let students know that they are lucky to have the unique perspectives that come from their cultures and that a language barrier is not a deficit. Communication is possible given a positive attitude and some effort.

▶ Take advantage of district translators.

Most districts have translators for parent conferences. Take a few minutes to request one. Try to schedule all conferences that require translation on the same day so a district translator can help facilitate these conferences back to back.

▶ Try out language translation applications.

These types of apps are getting more accurate every day. Today, they are almost spot on. Some suggestions include Google Translate, Talking Points, Remind, Bloomz, and Seesaw.

▶ Solicit help from your students.

Before making a phone call home, ask a student in your class how to say, "Is there someone in the household who speaks English? I am a teacher." When parents know that a teacher is calling, they will often make the effort to find a translator even if they have to get a neighbor to come over to help with the phone call.

▌ Schedule a conference over e-mail.

A parent almost always can get a relative, neighbor, or child to help translate a written message. Also, translating a written message may help relieve anxiety because the parent has time to find somebody to assist with translation and will not be put on the spot. Written communication is often preferred by parents who speak different languages. They, too, can use a language translating app if necessary.

▌ Have a backup plan.

Translators may not show up, may come late, or may be stretched too thin on parent conference day. There's nothing wrong with having two translators in one meeting. You can also consider asking the parents if they can bring someone who speaks both their language and English to the meeting. I've had many neighbors in my conferences who came to help out a parent. A really sweet touch is learning how to say "thank you" in the parent's home language before the meeting so you can put a smile on their face before they leave. It's also a sign that you respect their home language.

# Your Turn

1. How do you communicate with parents who speak a different language from you? Which of the tips above can you use to facilitate stronger communication?

2. What are your district and school policies on grading and late work? How can you make this information accessible to parents at your parent meetings?

3. How do you maintain low-density high-frequency communication with non-English-speaking parents? Do you use any applications or technology to assist?

# Managing Your Time Dealing With Extracurricular Activities

. . . . . . . . . . . . . . . . . . . . . . . . . . . . . . . . . . . . . . . . . . . . . . . .

If you are in your first two years of teaching, our advice is to focus on the commitments and responsibilities that go with your teaching role. Do not take on additional activities unless you are contracted to do so or just really want to.

For all teachers, we have two caveats: Know what you can control in your daily teaching/school life and don't be afraid to say "no" as a way of managing your time. According to Dr. Travis Bradberry, the author of the bestselling book *Emotional Intelligence 2.0* and the cofounder of TalentSmart, "Research conducted at the University of California in San Francisco shows that the more difficulty that you have saying no, the more likely you are to experience stress, burnout, and even depression, all of which erode self-control" (Bradberry, 2019). When it is necessary, learn to say "no" with skill—gracefully, gently, with respect, and with the understanding that you need to be in control of your workload in and out of school.

There were times during both of our teaching careers when we felt overworked but could not refuse taking on extra responsibilities such as coaching, advising a student club, helping our colleagues with their projects, working with students on community projects (see, for example, project-based learning), and special fundraising events. Your decision to engage in extracurricular activities, whatever they may be, should be based on your answers to these questions:

▶ How important is the activity to me and to others?

▶ How much time will I actually have for it?

▶ Who will I be helping?

▶ What will I need to do to accomplish the tasks?

▶ What is my expected timeline? A day, a week, a month, or longer?

▶ Is this something I must do? Why?

▶ Can I team up with others such as teachers, administrators, students, parents, and/or community organizations?

▶ Is there compensation (released time, financial rewards, etc.) for taking on this activity?

We have observed that teachers who are involved in extracurricular activities

▶ see themselves as more connected to the school and the school community;

▶ form bonds and have a better rapport and engagement with students;

▶ get to know students in a different atmosphere than a classroom;

▶ find that their involvement results in better student academic outcomes;

▶ receive deep appreciation from their school administration; and

▶ enjoy stronger connections with their colleagues.

The bottom line is that you will benefit from time spent participating in extracurricular activities.

Wisconsin superintendent Joe Sanfelippo has received a lot of national praise and recognition for implementing a program that acknowledges the hard work teachers do every day in and out of the classroom. In his 2019 Education Drive opinion piece, "4 Steps to Improving School Culture," Sanfelippo wrote,

We started doing a "Personal Day Giveaway" a few years ago. The process is relatively simple in that the week before the winter holiday break, we draw four names out of a hat, and our administrative team sets up a time with one of those four people to take over their job for the day. The staff member receives a personal day, and we assume their duties. The process has been great, but we started amplifying that work last year, and it took it to a completely new level. When we celebrated the work of the staff member publicly, the community got to see all the great things they were doing. Utilizing social media to celebrate their work allowed the community to commend that individual for their role in the school. (Sanfelippo, 2019)

## Your Turn

1. How would you assess your skill(s) in saying "no" to requests to take on tasks beyond teaching?

2. Was there anything we missed in the questions we asked? If, so what questions would you add?

3. Are these the questions that would help you and others make informed decisions about playing a role in extracurricular activities?

4. What did you think about the Wisconsin district rewarding teachers and staff? How might you modify the program for implementation in your school and/ or school district?

# STRATEGY #28

# Have a System to Keep Up With Your E-mails

*In 2019, the average office worker received 120 e-mails a day.*

*—Heinz Tschabitscher*

The difference between office workers and teachers is that we do not sit at a desk most of the day answering e-mails. We are teaching. Luckily, most of us are not receiving 120 e-mails a day, and much of the communication regarding our work comes in the form of hallway conversations with colleagues, face-to-face meetings, and face-to-face conversations with students. However, the e-mails from parents, colleagues, administration, and students still come daily. So how do we keep up?

Here's a rule of thumb for response time:

▶ **24-hour** turnaround for administration and colleagues. This keeps your school moving forward and is respectful toward your colleagues and administrators.

▶ **72-hour** turnaround for parents and students. Let them know this time frame at the beginning of the year.

Students are used to instant gratification, so you will have to set this professional boundary with them. It's also a good idea to give your students a mini-lesson or a template for appropriate language to use with teachers in an e-mail. This is a teachable moment; it is powerful knowledge for students to have for their educational career. It will also improve your experience when reading e-mails from students.

Many administrators and teachers come into work an hour early to tackle e-mails. Throughout the day they may monitor e-mails that come in, respond to a few after school, and then not look at e-mails again until the next morning (this last is true particularly for experienced teachers). If this works for you, we'd highly suggest using this strategy.

Tips for staying on top of your e-mails:

▶ Flag e-mails that you cannot attend to in the moment. Set aside a time during the week where you revisit your flagged e-mails. According to Heinz Tschabitscher (2019), "55.6% percent of e-mail is opened on mobile devices." In order to give the detailed responses that our flagged e-mails likely deserve, we should probably be responding to them on our desktops when we have the time and energy to focus on our responses. This means we need a system to keep track of them.

▶ Some e-mails are best answered in a phone call or conversation. If a parent is upset, call them. If a colleague is confused, go talk to them. Be aware that there can be lots of ambiguity with tone in an e-mail. Maintaining healthy relationships with colleagues and parents sometimes requires taking the time and effort necessary for a dialogue rather than a quick or one-sided e-mail. Conversations can clear up confusion faster and more effectively than e-mails.

▶ Advanced method: Use filter features in e-mail to have them automatically sorted into categories.

For heaven's sake, turn off your phone e-mail notifications. We mean it—do it right now. We're asking you to put down this book and turn them off now. Why? E-mail notifications make everything urgent, and everything is not urgent. *You* get to decide what is urgent. E-mail notifications also keep you in reactive mode.

Often we resort to text to get a faster response. Sometimes we text to tell someone we have sent them an e-mail. Unless it is a dire emergency, please refrain from doing this. It's telling the other person that your issue is more important than anything else they are doing at the time.

Set boundaries with e-mails. Be aware that if you make a practice of responding to e-mails on the weekend, parents and administration will come to expect a response on the weekend. Most experienced teachers know not to do this. We work hard enough during the week; try to make a practice of reserving your weekends for family time and your own personal rejuvenation. Other chapters in this book have covered the importance of spending time with friends and family and taking care of our mental health during the weekend. Most issues can wait. If there is an emergency, people know your phone number, but 99 percent of the time you do not need to spend time on the weekend responding to school issues. If a parent expects a response from you over the weekend, either by e-mail or phone, perhaps it's time to have a conversation with that parent to reset their expectations and confirm your boundaries.

## Your Turn

1. Do you have a system for staying on top of e-mails? Is that system working for you? Why or why not?

2. What strategy from this chapter could help you become even more efficient with e-mails?

3. When is a phone call more efficient and effective than writing or responding to an e-mail?

## STRATEGY #29

# Know When to Take Little Breaks Throughout the Day

- - - - - - - - - - - - - - - - - - - - - - - - - - - - - - - - - - - - - - - - - - - - - - - - -

*Almost everything will work again if you unplug it for a few minutes, including you.*

*—Anne Lamott*

Teaching is one of the professions that probably should have mandatory breaks. The medical profession is another, and it acknowledges this through its regulations. In order to ensure the highest quality of care for patients, Vanessa Patricelli explains that nurses scheduled for twelve-hour shifts are required to get a minimum of three fifteen-minute breaks and one uninterrupted meal period—and remember, that's only a minimum (Patricelli, 2016). Hospitals can be held liable if this does not happen. No matter how critical a patient is, the nurses are still forced to take a break. Hospitals know that nurses need uninterrupted break time to deal with the emotional and physical demands of providing high-quality care to patients. Without breaks, hospitals know that nurses are more likely to experience fatigue and burnout, and they could potentially make mistakes that severely affect the health of patients. Teachers also need to understand the importance of breaks and what effect they have on your performance, your mind, and your overall well-being. Sometimes we have to make our own breaks, and this might take some creativity.

[Serena] In my eighth-grade classroom, sometimes my only break through-out the day was lunch. We often had meetings during our prep that year. If our department didn't have a meeting, often there was a student meeting or a parent meeting, or perhaps a colleague's class needed to be covered at the last minute. This meant that the only time to use the restroom was in the min-utes between classes, and my only mental break was lunch.

I'm a person who needs to recharge alone. I know this about myself. I would put a paper over the window of my door (this is where I often saw two pair of little eyes peering in to see if I was inside the room), lock the door, and not answer if I heard any knocking. It didn't matter if it was a student or another teacher. I needed this twenty minutes or so to recharge so that I could be the teacher my students deserved for the other three periods of the day. Sometimes a school will take as much out of you as you can give. There was nowhere in the school I could go that would allow me private time. To clear my head, I would put on my Enya music (sometimes with headphones). Sometimes I would meditate, sometimes just breathe, and sometimes just sit there. A few times administrators would come in with their keys (they occasionally needed to check something in the classroom and didn't think I was inside) and find me sitting at my desk meditating like a monk. Luckily, my administrators under-stood what I was doing and didn't seem to mind. Often I would let them know not to tell the students I was inside the room. That was my little break.

[Ed] When I was principal, I found ways to take breaks. People seem to think that school leaders have the stamina of Superman or Superwoman, but we do not. Principals have many ways of taking a break or two on a daily basis. And principals *do* need breaks. Some of my methods included the following:

- Sometimes I spent at least fifteen minutes checking out the roof of the school to be sure "there were no leaks."

- I went to the janitor's room—few people go there.

- I closed the door to my office door—this tactic seldom worked, however.

- My favorite escape—I was a principal of two schools. One was a school with an elementary wing and a middle school wing on a single campus. The other school was a small K–4 school two miles away from the bigger and more challenging campus. So, guess where I went when I absolutely needed a break to maintain my sanity and temperament?

- After my usual lunch (a banana, an apple, and a candy bar), I would either visit the gym or run in the canyon behind the university. Noontime breaks (with exercise) achieved three things: (1) they provided a release from the pressures that go with most administrative jobs—they helped me put things in perspective, (2) they gave me release from tensions, and (3) they made me physically tired but more mentally alert.

## Your Turn

1. When can you carve out time to take breaks throughout the day?

2. Where will you take your break(s)?

3. How can breaks positively affect your time management?

# PART IV

## AT HOME

Illustration by Paper Scraps Inc.

*A friend of mine once told me that when she arrived at work and took off her coat, she realized that she was only wearing a slip. She had forgotten to get dressed, so she had to go home immediately. She was the secretary to the president of a college, so her job was stressful. No one saw her state of undress, but she obviously was so preoccupied from her stressful job that she had forgotten a major part of her outfit. She told her officemates that she had to run back home to drop off a key for the plumber.*

—*Melanie, licensed professional counselor*

# Manage Correspondence With Parents and Students

*When we fail to set boundaries and hold people accountable, we feel used and mistreated.*

*—Brene Brown*

Parents have one, two, or a few children. They spend their whole lives taking care of these children. It's a full-time job, and they are exhausted. You have 30 to 150 students. Let's say that three fourths of your students have two parents in the household (and we know that's being optimistic). That means you have 52 to 315 parents you correspond with each year. That's in addition to your students, who already take so much time and attention.

So, how can you manage all of these relationships? Set your boundaries early with your students and also with your parents. With today's technology, both students and parents have access to us after school. It's up to us to set our boundaries for when we will be available. It's difficult and can cause hurt feelings if we set a boundary later in the year after certain expectations have already been established. It's much easier to set and maintain realistic expectations from day one.

Heather Wolpert-Gawron (2019) summed it up nicely: "But we as professionals must love and care about ourselves, as well. Make sure that your needs are being met. School—especially for a new teacher—has a way of zapping your life force from you like a B-horror-movie succubus. Make sure you are doing what is necessary [to] protect your energy. It is not infinite."

What can happen when we stretch ourselves too thin mentally? It comes across to parents that we are unorganized and not in control, and we undersell the wonderful teachers we are. One of the teachers we spoke to, Linda Mello, the 2014 Golden Hill Elementary teacher of the year, had vivid memories of a time that happened. According to her, "One particularly stressful school year during parent teacher night, I introduced myself to a parent as Mrs. Miller. Then I said, 'Wait, no, that's not my name. It's Ms. Mello.' She probably thought I was an idiot or half in the bag." It happens to the best of us!

# Manage Correspondence With Students

With technology at their fingertips, students no longer have to wait until the morning to pop by your desk to ask for their grades. Most students have access to their grades 24/7. The issue is that a grading program can't explain why they received a B and not an A, or why they only earned 74 percent on the essay they thought they aced. That's when the questions start. If students have access to your e-mail address (which they do), they'll most likely ask via e-mail, and if they have access to your phone number (I'd advise against this) you may receive questions via texts. We suggest that you set boundaries with students early. But how? Catherine Beck, a middle and high school Spanish teacher in San Diego, shared her story with us in a personal communication:

I always encourage my students to communicate with me via e-mail if they are struggling with an independent assignment. I believe this does two things: First, it teaches students how to communicate effectively using technology; and second, it encourages them to seek out solutions to problems, as opposed to giving up or avoiding a difficult situation. This is especially important in urban education and with students from families who are struggling economically—95 percent of my students are on free or reduced lunch.

I first learned to use e-mail as an effective teaching tool when students started coming to class with incomplete homework assignments. Their homework was often incomplete because they didn't understand something about an assignment. I told them that they could always e-mail me as opposed to giving up. It was not long before I started receiving an overwhelming

*(Continued)*

(Continued)

number of e-mails from students asking me questions, telling me that they lost the assignment, asking about their grades, and requesting extensions. What had started as an exercise in self-advocacy and persistence became another way for students to avoid doing their homework. Meanwhile, I was unable to respond to the e-mails that were pouring in at all times of the day and night. The faster I responded to the e-mails, the more students expected of me.

I quickly realized that it was not enough to tell students to advocate for themselves. Students needed to be instructed about how to advocate for themselves using e-mail. They needed to learn how to write professional e-mails and what was considered an appropriate response time. Most importantly, I needed to set boundaries for my own sanity, so I made a new policy: "Please give me 24 hours to respond to your e-mails." I also reminded students that all e-mails received after 8:00 p.m would be answered the following day. The most important aspect to setting boundaries with the students was sticking to my own rules! If students e-mailed after 8:00 p.m., I did not respond until the next day. If the e-mail required a complicated response, I told students that they should come during tutoring hours so we could work out a solution together, as opposed to writing long e-mails with detailed content. Students quickly adapted to the new rules and learned to only e-mail me if it was truly necessary.

Whether you want to give yourself twenty-four or even forty-eight to seventy-two hours to respond to an e-mail, set some sort of boundaries for yourself. Why? Because you need to move the class forward as a whole and not get stuck on individual issues.

Another way to accomplish this goal is to let students know that you will only address grading questions during your office hours. You set the office hours that work best for you—it could be lunch one day of the week or after school twice a week. Post your office hours in your classroom, on your door, and in your e-mail signature. You decide what is best for you and what works for your class.

# Manage Correspondence With Parents

Jennifer Zimmermaker, a middle school special education teacher in the Poway Unified School District, sets her boundaries in a parent letter she sends home with students in the first week of school. Before she did this, she had parents texting her late into the night. She shared her letter with us.

Date: _____

Dear Parents,

Welcome back to _____ (school and program)! I am _____ and I am happy to have your child in my classroom and look forward to a great year. The following letter will clarify your basic questions about what my classroom collaboration model looks like, goals for the year, and what you will need to start the school year.

Our staff and students will be working together to meet the individual goals of each student. We will also address areas such as social skills, organization, character building, and group projects. It will be very important that parents read weekly announcements via e-mail and on the school website. I encourage our students to participate in all appropriate activities.

As a collaborative team, we have high expectations for all of our students. In addition to their IEP goals, we also have classroom standards as well as behavioral standards for all students. We encourage new skills daily and want to see social growth as well as academic growth. The following are our top priorities for the 2018–2019 school year:

1. **Communication**
   - The easiest way to contact me is through e-mail. My e-mail is _____ and my work phone number is _____. If you need to speak by phone, my office hours are until 4:30 p.m. from Monday–Friday. I am available to take calls during office hours and before school if needed. The best times to reach me are before and after school. I will not be available to respond to e-mails during the school day as I am busy helping students achieve their learning objectives, but I will respond to you as soon as I am able to. Thank you for your patience.

2. **Intensive work on IEP goals and essential core academics**
   - The main focus of each and every student is the IEP, which is a collective education tool prepared by the IEP team. It is our job to see that, to the best of our knowledge and abilities, the IEP is carried out as it is written. I have been reading your child's IEPs and am becoming familiar with their individual needs as well as their academic and social needs.

3. **Social skills training and independence**
   - This is an area that I feel very strongly about and will develop ways to integrate into a daily routine. Social interaction with classroom peers and school peers will be encouraged throughout the school day. In addition, school-wide independence at each student's level is also encouraged. We do social skills training daily as part of our curriculum. ****Lunch Buddies Club is recommended for all students. We will help them to participate at all levels.

*(Continued)*

Image by Suzanne Brill from Pixabay.

(Continued)

4. **Sensory and music integration**
   - All students have their own individual way of learning, and it is important to take into consideration these differences. My goal is to incorporate a multisensory approach to teaching so that all different levels of learning are touched upon.

5. **Nutrition break**
   - We also have a nutrition break every day, so make sure to pack a snack in your child's backpack.

If you have an e-mail address and it is a good mode of communication for you, please feel free to e-mail with any additional questions you may have. I am looking forward to meeting you all and getting to know your children. This is going to be a great school year!

Sincerely,

The bottom line is it's difficult to set boundaries only after you realize you need them. It's much easier to set them at the beginning of the year and refer back to them when needed. Make them part of your first-week introduction to your classroom (see *Real Talk About Classroom Management*, "First Days of School"). Post them in your room. You'll thank yourself in November.

## Your Turn

1. Do your students have access to their grades? What system resonates with you for answering grade-related questions?

2. How can you set boundaries with parents and students and still maintain healthy correspondence?

3. What after-work boundaries do you personally need with parents and students? (Remember, everybody is different.)

# STRATEGY #31

# Taking Care of Yourself

. . . . . . . . . . . . . . . . . . . . . . . . . . . . . . . . . . . . . . . . . . . . . .

*In order for you to take care of your classroom, you have to take care of yourself. Eat right, exercise, and get enough sleep. You need a body–mind–spirit balance.*

—*Serena Pariser*

"I have so much to do that there isn't enough time for self-care." We've all said this to ourselves. You have to make time. Almost nobody has time for self-care, but some people manage to carve out time for it. People who take care of their mind, body, and spirit perform better at work. They are filling their cup.

More and more research is being generated about the benefits of self-care. How are you doing right now? Here is our self-care checklist with implications of what you must do.

1. How often do you skip daily exercise?

   _____ Very often          _____ Sometimes          _____ Almost never

2. Are you getting enough sleep?

   _____ Most of the time          _____ Could use more

3. Do you drink enough water each day?

   _____ I try to          _____ I need to do better

4. How often do you find yourself relying on caffeine to get through the day?

   _____ Very often          _____ On occasion          _____ Not often

5. How often do you skip breakfast and/or lunch and rely on junk food?

   _____ Very often          _____ Sometimes          _____ Almost never

6. Do you schedule or partake in downtime activities each week?          Yes          No

   If yes, list your three favorite downtime activities.

   a) _____          b) _____          c) _____

7. How would you rate your ability to delegate tasks to students in your classroom?

   _____ Could be better          _____ Really good

8. How would you rate your skill at saying "no" to doing things that you don't care about or that will take time away from your primary teacher's tasks?

   _____ I'm good at it          _____ I need to learn how to do it better

9. How well do you handle emotions like fear, sadness, or worry?

   _____ I think I handle them well          _____ I need to work on doing better

10. Are you a person who is curious about things and enjoys exploring new ideas, skills, and people?

    _____ Yes, that's me!          _____ It depends on a variety of factors          _____ Not for me

11. How would you rate your skills in speaking up about events and issues that bother you at school?

    _____ Not good at this     _____ Need help to do this     _____ I seldom hesitate to express my opinions

12. How would you rate your sense of humor?

    _____ Poor          _____ Good          _____ Excellent

13. How would you rate the quality of the social interactions and relationships you have at school, outside of school, and in life in general?

    School: _____ Excellent     _____ Good     _____ Fair     _____ Not good at all

    Outside: _____ Excellent     _____ Good     _____ Fair     _____ Not good at all

    Life: _____ Excellent     _____ Good     _____ Fair     _____ Not good at all

There are tips you can use to help you with each item on the self-care checklist. Share these tips with your teaching colleagues (and even noneducators).

[Serena] If I'm stressed about something and I try to forget about it, I get a knot in my stomach before I go to sleep. It doesn't go away and makes it difficult to fall asleep. I found that warming a hot water bottle and holding it on my stomach puts me right to sleep. There's something about heat that relaxes both our body and our mind. I always sleep through the night and wake up feeling refreshed. However, the fact that the knot is there means that my body is telling me something is off.

Everybody has a different way their body may be hinting to them to step up the self-care. What's yours?

## Your Turn

1. Did this checklist help increase your awareness of how your emotions and beliefs drive your thinking, influence your behavior, and affect your judgment? If so, how?

2. Would you agree that being more self-reflective helps you keep grounded by slowing down your thinking and emotional processes? If so, how and when do you schedule your thinking time?

3. What items would you add to this checklist?

4. How does your body tell you when you need more self-care? Do you listen? Why or why not?

# Meditation

. . . . . . . . . . . . . . . . . . . . . . . . . . . . . . . . . . . . . . . . . . . . . . . . .

*You don't have to believe in [meditation] for it to work.*

*—Russell Simmons, hip-hop mogul*

When some of us think of meditation we might conjure an image of a thin Buddhist monk in an orange robe, sitting in the lotus position with his eyes closed, softly chanting. While meditation can look like this for some, it can also take on a myriad of other forms. Businesspeople meditate, world leaders meditate, harried stay-at-home parents meditate, and teachers meditate—sometimes for a few stolen minutes between classes. Many people are quickly realizing the astounding benefits that a consistent practice of meditation can bring to their lives.

Additionally, companies are starting to learn the powerful benefits meditation can provide in terms of increased patience, focus, and clarity. In fact, billionaire Ray Dalio reported, "Meditation more than anything in my life was the biggest ingredient of whatever success I had" (Gregoire, 2017). A number of Fortune 500 companies are bringing meditation directly into the workplace. What could happen if we brought meditation to schools? After all, as teachers, we need all of the same benefits as businesspeople—every period, every day.

Former president Barak Obama has a daily meditation practice, as do many other powerful leaders. Some do it for productivity, some for clarity, and others because they know it is essential to keep the mind strong when going about their demanding high-stress jobs. Here is a list of some well-known people who meditate, as reported in Gregoire (2017):

▶ Oprah Winfrey, chairwoman and CEO of Harpo Productions—meditates twenty minutes a day

▶ Jerry Seinfeld—meditates daily for creativity

▶ Padmasree Warrior, CTO of Cisco—meditates every night for calmness and clarity

▶ Tony Schwartz, founder and CEO of The Energy Project—claims meditation has freed him from migraines and helped him develop patience

▶ Bill Ford, executive chairman of Ford Motor Company—learned to develop compassion for himself though meditation practice

▶ Robert Stiller, CEO of Green Mountain Coffee Roasters—practices meditation for better task focus and accomplishment; has a meditation room at the company headquarters in Vermont

▶ Ariana Huffington, president and editor in chief of Huffington Post Media Group— brought meditation into her company and offers weekly classes for both AOL and Huffington Post Media employees

▶ Russell Simmons, hip-hop mogul—practices transcendental meditation

These are people who need to have their brain in tip-top shape every day. They have found that meditation is an essential part of their daily routine.

You are an educator. That means you are a powerful leader, facilitator, counselor, disciplinarian, friend, and colleague. You make endless decisions each day, remember so much, and have so many students to keep track of. Meditation can and will help. One university president we spoke with said, "I try to meditate every day. I try to keep it lock solid. When I don't, I find I'm not as patient." There are so many different types of ways to meditate. They all work. Find the one that resonates with you. We suggest you start meditating now and form the habit before you reach a point where you are so mentally cluttered, anxious, and exhausted that you're grasping at any remedy available.

Starting a meditation practice can be tough. It's hard to schedule it in or find time to do it. Getting started will be the toughest part. The first few times you might find your mind drifting, and that's okay. Be kind with yourself. The best is yet to come. Over time (maybe two weeks), if you mediate daily you may start to notice the following benefits:

▶ Improved patience

▶ Improved feelings of joy

▶ Improved ability to clear your mind on demand before classes

▶ Improved impulse control

▶ Feeling more present during class

▶ A sense of calmness

▶ An increase in creativity

▶ An increase in productivity

▶ Lowered stress levels

▶ Improved cognitive functioning

▶ Improved mental health

We're not saying you shouldn't meditate simply to clear your mind and relax, but when you start a regular meditation practice, you will find that the *proactive* benefits will start to outweigh the calming *reactive* benefits. For example:

▶ Do you tend to overreact when a child acts out? Meditation will proactively help.

▶ Do you feel overwhelmed when you are asked to do a new task? Meditation will proactively help.

▶ Do you tend to be so overwhelmed with things to do that you forget things? Meditation will proactively help.

▶ Do you have trouble keeping all of your tasks in order? Meditation will proactively help.

Meditation helps with your reactive system and helps you achieve your optimal brain potential. We have too much to do to not be operating at optimal capacity.

To realize the benefits of meditation, you should practice it almost every day and ideally at the same time each day. First thing in the morning is most beneficial if that is realistic for you. There are free apps available that can guide you through; just keep earbuds next to your desk or by your bed and pop them in for the first few minutes of each day or for a few minutes during your prep.

Some meditation apps you might want to try out are Headspace, Insight Timer, Glo, Calm, and Ten Percent Happier.

According to an article on the website of Sonorrari, a company that promotes the calming and healing powers of sound,

> Studies have shown that [meditation] can actually change the way our brains processes information and manages the effects of stress, depression, and anxiety. Those who practice meditation, research has demonstrated, are happier and calmer than their counterparts who don't, so it's no surprise that many high-stress businesses are catching on and making meditation a part of their corporate mission." (Sonorrari, 2017)

The article lists the following well-known companies that provide on-site meditation for all of their employees:

- Apple—Apple employees are granted thirty minutes a day to meditate. Apple provides a meditation room and offers on-site classes on meditation and yoga.

- Prentice Hall Publishing—provides a meditation space in headquarters

- Google—has a meditation space on-site; offers a company-wide meditation program so that employees can learn how to meditate

- Nike—provides a meditation room on-site

- AOL Time Warner—after downsizing, the company added meditation classes and a meditation room to help employees de-stress and focus

- Yahoo!—provides a meditation room on-site

- Proctor and Gamble—provides a meditation room on-site

- HBO—provides meditation classes in the workplace

Even if your school does not provide an on-site mediation room, you can still meditate in your classroom, in your (parked) car, and/or at home.

Consider also that "when teachers are stressed and not coping well, the relationships they have with students are likely to suffer, leading to negative academic and behavioral outcomes for students" (Herman, Hickmon-Rosa, and Reinke, 2017, p. 91). Bringing the conversation back to time management, when our minds are preforming better, our relationships with students strengthen, we will be more patient, and we will show up to school more present. This will save us time in the long run. In her 2016 article, "Change and the Uncluttered Mind," Melissa Bell wrote,

We have somehow convinced ourselves that being stressed out is normal, and may actually be good for our productivity. Actually, the opposite is true. Stress is not normal; it is an imbalance experienced in the body when the stress system is chronically activated. Stress is neither necessary nor inevitable. Our minds and bodies seek homeostasis—balance. That is what's natural, and that is what works. Likewise, our minds need to be in balance, not in turmoil. We seek and need mental clarity. (Bell, 2016)

We are the CEOs of our classrooms. The benefits experienced by meditating teachers are astounding, yet not surprising. Summarizing a 2014 study, an article by the Maharishi University of Management quoted Dr. Charles Elder, who explained,

The results of this randomized controlled trial are very striking and demonstrate the utility of introducing a stress reduction program for teachers and other public and private employees. The four-month study found significant and clinically important decreases in perceived stress, emotional exhaustion associated with teacher burnout, and depressive symptoms in those practicing the TM [transcendental meditation] program compared to a wait-list control group. (Elder, 2014)

Meditation is especially helpful in the notoriously stressful times of the year, such as right before breaks or at the end of the school year. Sometimes when we don't feel like meditating is when we need it the most.

Try these tips for meditating:

▶ Meditate for three to five minutes when you first wake up and before bed.

▶ Meditate after school to release stress and calm your mind.

▶ Ask your principal to set aside a quiet part of the school (away from students) as a meditation room for just teachers and staff.

▶ Use online tools such as YouTube or apps to guide yourself through meditation.

▶ Have a meditation accountability partner.

Surprisingly enough, when we asked around we had a hard time finding teachers who had a daily mediation practice. Every teacher we asked was curious or admitted they needed to start, but few had developed the habit.

Being less reactive and more patient means being more engaged with your students. This means more energy to get things done and focus on what really matters.

## Your Turn

1. Do you think a daily meditation practice could help save you time? If so, how?

2. Realistically speaking, what time of day do you think it would be most beneficial for you to meditate?

3. Do you know anybody who practices meditation daily? How does it affect their life?

# STRATEGY #33

# Enjoy Your Time After School and on the Weekends

*It is definitely possible to have a balanced work and personal life, but it's difficult because work can be so stressful and consuming. During student teaching, my master teacher taught me some tips for balancing work and personal life. During the weekend, she brings her school laptop home, but not the charger. She'll work on lesson planning and other school stuff until the laptop dies, and then she stops. I like this strategy because it forces you to prioritize and do only the important things since you only have a limited amount of time. This practice, in addition to doing something fun over the weekend, made my master teacher happy and refreshed on Monday mornings.*

*—A new teacher*

There's always going to be something else that needs to get done. That's the nature of teaching. It's up to us to set our own limits and understand what truly needs to be done to make our classrooms and schools function successfully. Author Anne Lamott stated it beautifully when she said, "Almost everything else will work again if you unplug it for a few minutes, including you" (Clements, 2015).

First- and second-year teachers often find themselves working more hours than experienced teachers. That's natural and it's okay. It *does* get easier, we promise you. In order to have time on weeknights and weekends to recharge, we have to work smarter during the day. Every other chapter in this book focuses on working smarter. This chapter focuses on why and how to enjoy our time after school and on the weekends.

---

[Serena] When I taught a graduate-level classroom management class to student teachers, I used to do an assignment in one of the classes where I asked the student teachers to do something that energized them. I suggested that the activity have the following characteristics:

- The activity should be something they genuinely enjoyed doing.

- The activity should be done either by themselves or with people they did not work or have class with.

- They were not to talk about work or school during the activity.

- They should choose an activity that gave them energy—this could be anything from hiking to drawing to going to the beach to camping or even having a picnic.

- They were to do this activity the day before they taught the next day.

- They were to take a picture of themselves doing the activity.

The second part of the assignment was to report back on the quality of their classroom management the day after the energizing activity. One of my students chose to go surfing. Another chose to go to an outdoor yoga class. Another chose to spend time with her family for a dinner that she often missed on Sundays. And another chose to simply go to the beach to pick up seashells that she liked. Regardless of the activity, the results were all the same. They reported feeling refreshed and more patient with the students, and in turn the students were more engaged in the learning the next day. After the assignment, many wished they had taken more time to recharge when they needed it most throughout the year. The last part of the assignment was to hang the picture near their desk or put it inside their desk somewhere to remind them to recharge when needed. I urge you to do the same!

---

Why are we waiting so long to recharge? Why do we often forget about ourselves during the school year? The time is now. Give yourself permission to enjoy your time after school and on the weekends. Teaching is a marathon, not a sprint. We don't want you to burn out before the race is over.

When we take time to recharge:

▶ We show up more present for our students the next day or after the weekend.

▶ We do not feel resentment toward our class for sacrificing our personal time.

▶ We have more to give.

▶ We are more excited about our lessons and, in turn, our students are more engaged.

▶ We give our brains a break from the teaching thoughts that go through our heads.

▶ We'll work faster after we recharge because we will be more refreshed and refocused—it's a win-win.

The happiest and most successful teachers know this. They most likely travel or spend time with their family and friends over breaks and perhaps even during the week for dinners and get-togethers. The happiest teachers don't blur the lines when they are doing what energizes them. The happiest and most successful teachers also probably learned this through feeling the pain of not recharging. Learn how to recharge early in your career. Turn off your work e-mail and really enjoy your time off. If you need to log in to e-mail for just small chunks of time, that's fine. Perhaps you can take a short walk before grading papers. Or perhaps you can reward yourself by trying that new Brazilian restaurant with a friend after you finish creating an assessment.

Joining an organized sports or recreational league is another effective way to recharge. Other activities that can work to force you to unplug are book clubs, cooking groups, or even a group game night. If you join a group that gets you moving, even better. Having a group of people who rely on you to show up will force you to unplug on those scheduled evenings and weekends.

---

[Serena] I personally recharge when I'm in nature. I go camping to recharge or take day trips into nature. Often before a camping trip I feel like I have so much to do. I think about backing out of the trip and just staying home to catch up. While I am recharging I make it a point not to talk about work or students. If these topics come up, I make myself purposefully and gently change the subject. I need to do this because as much as I love my students and the work I do, once I start thinking about it I have trouble turning off the thoughts. To be a better educator, I know I need to recharge. My brain needs a rest. So does yours. When I return from my nature trips, I'm twice as productive the next week. My brain is ready to go, and I have a huge smile on my face.

Our minds will trick us into thinking we don't need to recharge. The most content and successful people we know, in any profession, choose not to talk about work when they are recharging. You may have the tendency to feel guilty when you decide to take time out for yourself rather than do another task for your classroom. We get it. We're not saying to unplug your computer every day at 4 p.m. until the next morning and every weekend, all weekend. What we are suggesting is that you make sure you take time for yourself after school some evenings and on the weekends for at least one day. You don't have to be a martyr to be passionate about your classroom.

Your students need a teacher who is present, who smiles, and who is energized and ready for them. They need you at your best—both you and your class deserve that. The last thing students need is a teacher who was up all night grading papers and is now chugging coffee to get through the lesson (and most likely telling them how she or he was up all night grading papers). If you do need to grade or plan during nights and weekends, then do it efficiently and with minimal distractions so you can leave a bit of time for yourself to recharge. This takes responsibility on your part. This means that by Friday afternoon, you should have completed your lesson plan for the upcoming week. If you *do* need to take a few papers home for the weekend to grade, however, we forgive you. The goal is to work efficiently and contentiously so that eventually you don't have to grade over the weekend. Use your preps wisely. It's worth it.

Serena unplugging on a camping trip in Anza-Borrego Springs.

## Your Turn

1. If you had the time, what would you do that energizes you?

2. Do you have a hobby that you have given up in the past few years? Can you come up with a plan to restart that hobby?

3. Come up with a plan to carve out time to do the thing that allows you to unplug and energizes you so that you will be more present for your students. What might that plan look like? Optional: Share your plan with an accountability partner so your partner can ask you the following week if you've followed through with it.

# STRATEGY #34

# Secondary Trauma

*Nothing can wear you out like caring about people.*

—S.E. Hinton

[Serena] When I taught eighth grade, I had a student—we'll call him Mark. I had a soft spot for Mark. He was smaller than the other boys and always seemed to be having a giggle about something. He loved to skate but didn't seem to have any other hobbies. He had the street smarts of a twenty-year-old, easily. He didn't particularly love academics and held a steady F in my class most of the year. At one point, he and I worked together to guide him up to a C-. He beamed and bragged that this was a highlight in his academic career. Regardless of his grades, I liked him. He would joke with me often, and although he was less than interested in academics, we had a strong connection and a mutual respect for each other. This is the foundation for connecting with any student academically. I found Mark particularly funny. He had a contagious energy about him, and he brought a smile to his classmates' faces. I had an attachment to Mark. I can't put my finger on why.

Although Mark was excited about earning a C- in my English class that one semester, I knew the work wasn't done. I had bigger plans for Mark academically. Mark had very high emotional intelligence. He knew exactly how to get under any teacher's skin. I was thankful he hadn't chosen me as a victim. I'm not sure exactly what he did in his mathematics and science classes, but

*(Continued)*

(Continued)

I found him constantly in the dean's office during those periods. He would give me a peace sign, raise his eyebrows, and flash a big smile as I walked by on my way to prep.

I had Mark in my first period, so I was lucky to be able to connect with him first thing in the morning, before everything seemed to spiral downward for him. One day Mark did not show up to class. I asked his girlfriend where he was, as she seemed to keep better tabs on him then his parents. She looked down and didn't respond at first. My stomach dropped. Then she said she hadn't heard from him, either.

A few days later Mark's girlfriend came up to my desk. She said Mark had made some very poor decisions and was at the wrong place at the wrong time. He had been involved with an attempted car theft. Mark was in juvenile detention and would be there for a while.

The day went by, and on my drive home I started crying. The tears poured down my face. I started sobbing so hard I could barely drive. This surprised me because I rarely cry sad tears; I tend to manage my emotions well. I imagined little Mark surrounded by teenagers much larger than he was. He wouldn't get by with his jokes there. Deep down, I knew that he probably wasn't going to make it. I thought he might end up in jail, and I couldn't save him. I never saw Mark again. To this day, I do not know where Mark is and have not heard anything further about him.

That evening, after I wiped away the tears, I felt heavy. I lay down in my bed and slept. Sleeping is all I had the energy to do because of the weight of the heavy emotions I was experiencing. It was only 5 p.m.

---

At the time of this incident, I didn't know what was happening. I thought it was a normal part of teaching and I was just upset about a student. Now I know that what I was experiencing is commonly referred to as *secondary trauma*. According to the National Child Trauma Stress Network (n.d.), "Secondary trauma is defined as the emotional duress that results when an individual hears about a firsthand trauma experience of another."

Sixty-seven percent of our students have experienced trauma. If you work with high-needs students, the number is probably larger. There's a pretty good chance some of these students are going to tell us about their trauma or we are going to be their teacher when it happens. As much as we love our students—our Marks—we need to take care of ourselves. The rest of the class still needs us to be centered, focused, caring, and compassionate teachers. If we aren't aware of secondary trauma before we step into the classroom, it's more than likely that we will silently suffer from it without knowing what is happening.

Why did we decide to add a chapter on secondary trauma in a time management book? It's simple: If we are experiencing secondary trauma, we aren't performing at our optimal level. We can't perform the way we need to if we are experiencing secondary trauma. The issue is that you care about your students. When we are suggesting ways to prevent compassion fatigue, we are helping you stay strong because you still have the rest of the class to teach and your families to take care of at home. It's okay to feel good and still care about your other students.

## Prevention

We can strengthen our minds and bodies *before* we hear about traumatic events. Methods for this can include but are not limited to the following:

▶ Meditation—you'll notice that meditation is a common theme in this book. Yes, it will strengthen our ability to regulate our emotions and actually "pad" our brain to be able to better process. Let's get more meditation rooms in schools! Teachers need it.

▶ Exercise—a strong body has a better ability to regulate emotions.

▶ Nutrition

▶ Yoga

▶ School counselors can give presentations to staff about secondary trauma or compassion fatigue to increase awareness.

▶ School leaders can be trained on secondary trauma.

## Intervention

If you have been exposed to secondary trauma, you need to get it out of your body. Keep in mind that it can be difficult to tell if something is secondary trauma or if we are just tired from the day. Here are some ways to get secondary trauma out of your body:

▶ Practice yoga.

▶ Use employee assistance programs (EAPs) if you are experiencing secondary trauma.

▶ Enlist a self-care partner to help monitor your progress.

▶ Get out into nature.

▶ Go exercise (a.k.a. gym therapy).

▶ Journal it out.

▶ Talk to your school counselor about strategies.

▶ Talk it out. (Be careful with this one—a counselor or therapist is best for talking it out so we don't spread the secondary trauma to others.)

▶ Talk into a voice recorder on your phone; delete the recording when you are finished.

▶ Dance it out.

You may think our suggestion to dance sounds morbidly distasteful. We aren't suggesting a celebratory dance. Dancing, in many cultures, is a way people heal from trauma. Some even find it more effective than professional counseling. After the horrific genocide in Rwanda, professionally trained mental health experts from the West volunteered their services. The reaction of the Rwandans surprised many. According to author Andrew Solomon,

[The Western experts'] practice did not involve being outside in the sun where you begin to feel better. There was no music or drumming to get your blood flowing again. There was no sense that everyone had taken the day off so that the entire community could come together to try to lift you and bring you joy. Instead they would take people one at a time into these dingy little rooms and have them sit around for an hour or so and talk about bad things that had happened to them. We had to ask them to leave. (Solomon, 2009)

On the television show *Grey's Anatomy*, the two main characters from season one, Dr. Meredith Grey and Dr. Cristina Yang, often "danced it out" when stress levels reached almost unbearable levels at the hospital. Even successful surgeons (okay, *television* surgeons) know that dancing can help! The point is whether you dance, talk to a friend, journal it out, or do some sort of exercise, don't fall asleep. You need to get it out.

Counselors and therapists are trained in this. Unfortunately, most of the time teachers are not. While doing research for this book, we found people in all professions who shared their stories of secondary trauma. We heard from people who work with seriously sick children, veterans of war, caretakers who work with trauma every day, and medical professionals who deal with families suffering from grief and loss. Treating secondary trauma appropriately is especially important for teachers because, as mentioned earlier, 67 percent of the students we work with have been exposed to some sort of trauma. The chances of us experiencing secondary trauma are high. And we work with children—*children*! Let's give them what they deserve.

The danger of not getting out trauma if you are exposed is that it will affect your time management negatively. Your brain and body won't be performing at an optimal level. Secondary trauma can cause us to forget things, feel lethargic, and be on edge.

## Your Turn

1.  Have you experienced secondary trauma? What did it feel like in your body?

2.  What preventative strategies can you adopt to strengthen your mind and body to help prevent compassion fatigue?

3.  If you were to experience secondary trauma, what strategies would you use to get it out of your body?

# STRATEGY #35

# Compassion Fatigue

The best way we can think to describe what compassion fatigue looks like is to consider the DMV. Although it's really no fault of their own, the DMV (in most cities) is an organization that exudes compassion fatigue. DMV employees work countless hours, often without exposure to sunlight, dealing with people who are frustrated and whose problems are all different from one another. One DMV worker listens to more than fifty issues a day. DMV employees experience people getting really *really* upset daily, often at them. Frequently they come across as lacking compassion, and when we are there seeking their services, we often feel like we are being treated as just a number rather than as a person. We are asked to sit on rock-hard seats as we wait for (sometimes) hours to get a few minutes of numb, robotic conversation and little eye contact. We doubt DMV workers started out like this.

Caretakers such as doctors, teachers, or family members can also show the effects of compassion fatigue. One doctor of pulmonary and critical care medicine we interviewed described it by saying, "Compassion fatigue is not just numbness. It becomes irritation and exasperation with people who are suffering." Dr. F. Oshburg explains further: "Compassion fatigue develops over time—taking weeks, sometimes years to surface. Basically, it's a low level, chronic clouding of caring and concern for others in your life. . . . Over time, your ability to feel and care for others becomes eroded through overuse of your skills of compassion" (American Institute of Stress, 2018).

Most equate the high turnover of employees at the DMV to the lack of competitive wages, but we'd like to argue it's also the nature of the job itself. Hour after hour people complain to DMV workers, often screaming in their faces. Like DMV workers, teachers can sometimes feel this level of compassion fatigue.

However, as teachers we're working with children. We can't afford to lose our compassion or empathy or allow ourselves to feel constantly irritated. Children need us to model healthy coping skills.

Unlike secondary trauma where we hurt because we've heard about someone else's pain, with compassion fatigue we *stop caring* as a defense mechanism for survival. As teachers we need to take measures to prevent and overcome compassion fatigue because our students need us to be the compassionate, caring advocates we started out as. Their minds are young, malleable, sensitive, and impressionable. They need our positivity and love daily to grow up to be mentally healthy adults. Some of our students spend more time with us during the school year than with their parents or close friends. We can't adequately raise the next generation if our minds are numb.

In terms of time management, suffering from compassion fatigue may cause us to lose ambition, stagnate, lose the meaning in our work, and experience a decrease in our cognitive ability. A happy brain will manage time better and be more efficient.

> [Ed] When Serena and I meet, we laugh often. It seems the more we laugh the sharper our brains become and the more we get done in the meeting. Sometimes we have meetings where one of us is upset. In those meetings we rarely finish our agenda items, our creativity is decreased, and we work much slower. There's a mental block.

The difference between the advice for dealing with compassion fatigue and for dealing with secondary trauma is that you are not "getting it out" when dealing with compassion fatigue. When you experience compassion fatigue, you'll need to manage your health over the long run for prevention of future occurrences. Some suggestions for managing compassion fatigue include the following:

- Talk to somebody.
- Exercise and eat properly.
- Get enough sleep.
- Take a personal day.
- Spend time with family or close friends.

❱ Take a break from grading for a weekend.

❱ Develop interests outside of work.

Mother Theresa understood compassion fatigue. The American Institute of Stress (2018) reported that "[Mother Theresa] wrote in her plan to her superiors that it was *mandatory* for her nuns to take an entire year off from their duties every 4–5 years to allow them to heal from the effects of their care-giving work."

## Your Turn

1. Do you think there have been some months during the school year that you suffered from compassion fatigue? Describe what happened. Looking back, what could you have done differently to prepare yourself or to prevent this from happening?

2. How are the remedies for secondary trauma and compassion fatigue similar and different from one another?

3. What is your take on the relationship between time management and compassion fatigue?

# An Open Letter to All Teachers After Reading This Book

· · · · · · · · · · · · · · · · · · · · · · · · · · · · · · · · · · · · · · · · · ·

*Teachers,*

*There are moments in the day when you make important time management decisions. The tiny moments in the day when you decide to focus, to meditate, to use technology or not use technology, to be present, to tackle paperwork differently, or to finish the e-mails you started. The moments when you make those decisions are where the true power of time management comes into play. You have control of your workload, your classroom, your life, and your responsibilities.*

*Now that you have strategies to be a powerful time manager, you will notice that you start to accomplish more and have a sense of calm and control over your classroom (most days). It's so important to take time to stop and celebrate your accomplishments. If you just keep plowing through, you won't appreciate how far you've come. Celebrate with a loved one when you get that stack of papers graded. Celebrate with a massage when you finish a unit. Celebrate with a friend when you get caught up with your e-mails. Celebrate with a colleague when you get your classroom decluttered. Celebrate by going to the park and simply relaxing after you successfully conquered time management in groupwork in a lesson. These are all accomplishments!*

*Now that you have these tools and strategies, it's up to you to make a decision to have more energy, to be happier, to be more present, and to be your best self in and out of the classroom. You deserve this. We've given you thirty-five strategies, but there are more. The magic of these strategies reveals itself in the moments when you make decisions on how to manage your time. If you don't, your time and workload will manage you.*

*When you come across an obstacle or find yourself overworked or dragging your feet, flip back through this book. Is there something in it that can help you? What is stopping you from being the best teacher you can be? What is stopping you from having more personal time and more time with loved ones?*

*If you are reading this book, you are most likely in the 95 percent of teachers who love your job. We love you for this. The students need you in the classroom. You deserve to feel good every day and be the teacher who you imagined when you were sitting in your teacher certification classes. We believe in you. You got this.*

*Go get 'em!*

*Serena and Ed*

# References

Academic Success for All Learners. (n.d.). The research literature: Time management. Retrieved from http://iseesam.com/content/teachall/text/effective/research/time.pdf

American Institute of Stress. (2018). Compassion fatigue. Retrieved from https://www.stress.org/military/for-practitionersleaders/compassion-fatigue

Badass Teachers Association. (2017). 2017 Educator Quality of Life Work Survey. Retrieved from https://www.aft.org/sites/default/files/2017_eqwl_survey_web.pdf

Bell, M. (2016). Change and the uncluttered mind. Retrieved from https://www.linkedin.com/pulse/change-uncluttered-mind-melissa-bell/

Berger, R. (2012). *Austin's butterfly: Building excellence in student work* [Video file]. Retrieved from https://vimeo.com/38247060

Boogren, T. (2016). Teachers are master multi-taskers. Retrieved from https://everydayteacherstyle.com/2016/09/07/teachers-are-master-multi-taskers-but-we-already-knew-that/

Bourdo, C. (2019). The biggest lesson of my first year teaching. Retrieved from https://www.edutopia.org/article/biggest-lesson-my-first-year-teaching

Bradberry, T. (2014). Multitasking damages your brain and career, new studies suggest. Retrieved from https://www.forbes.com/sites/travisbradberry/2014/10/08/multitasking-damages-your-brain-and-career-new-studies-suggest/#5b9d7b7256ee

Bradberry, T. (2019). How successful people stay productive and in control. Retrieved from https://www.talentsmart.com/articles/How-Successful-People-Stay-Productive-and-In-Control-898862998-p-1.html

Brown, B. (2010). *The gifts of imperfection*. Center City, MN: Hazeldon Publishing.

Byrne, U. (2008). If you want something done, ask a busy person. *Business Information Review 25*(3), 190–196.

Caolo, D. (2014). The benefits of being organized. Retrieved from https://unclutterer.com/2014/01/23/benefits-of-being-organized/

Cherry, K. (2019, November 12). Understanding the psychology of positive thinking. *VeryWellMind*. Retrieved from https://www.verywellmind.com/what-is-positive-thinking-2794772

Clements, E. (2015). "Every single thing I know, as of today": Author Anne Lamott shares life wisdom in viral Facebook post. Retrieved from https://www.today.com/popculture/author-anne-lamott-shares-life-wisdom-viral-facebook-post-t13881

Donahoo, L., Siegrist, B., & Garrett-Wright, D. (2018). Addressing compassion fatigue and stress of special education teachers and professional staff using mindfulness and prayer. Retrieved from https://www.ncbi.nlm.nih.gov/pubmed/28812432

Elder, C., Nidich, S., Moriarty, F., & Nidich, R. (2018). The effects of transcendental meditation on employee stress, depression, and burnout: A randomized controlled study. Retrieved from http://www.thepermanentejournal.org/issues/2014/winter/5591-transcendental-meditation.html

Elliott, K., Elliott, J., & Spears, S. (2018). Teaching on empathy. As more students suffer from trauma, compassion fatigue is becoming a problem for teachers and administrators alike. *Principal Magazine*. Retrieved from https://www.naesp.org/sites/default/files/Elliottetal_ND18.pdf

Goodenow, C. (1993). Classroom belonging among early adolescent students: Relationships to motivation and achievement. *Journal of Early Adolescence,13*, 21–43.

Gregoire, C. (2017). The daily habit of these outrageously successful people. Retrieved from https://www.huffpost.com/entry/business-meditation-executives-meditate_n_3528731

Hattie, J. (2008). *Visible learning: A synthesis of over 800 meta-analyses relating to student achievement*. Milton Park, United Kingdom: Routledge.

Hattie, J. (2018). 250+ influences on student achievement. Retrieved from https://us.corwin.com/sites/default/files/250_influences_chart_june_2019.pdf

Herman, K. C., Hickmon-Rosa, J., & Reinke, W. M. (2017). Empirically derived profiles of teacher stress, burnout, self-efficacy, and coping and associated student opinions. *Journal of Positive Behavior Interventions, 20*(2), 90–100.

James, H. (2015). 3 simple ways to manage teacher workload stress. Retrieved from http://blog.whooosreading.org/simple-ways-to-manage-teacher-workload-stress/

Jennings, P., &Greenberg M. T. (2009). The prosocial classroom: Teacher social and emotional competence in relation to student and classroom outcomes. *Review of Educational Research, 79*(1), 491–525.

Leroy, S. (2009). Why is it so hard to do my work? Retrieved from https://www.sciencedirect.com/science/article/pii/S0749597809000399

Lin, L., Cockerham, D., & Chang, Z. (2015). Task speed and accuracy decrease when multitasking. Retrieved from https://www.researchgate.net/publication/283789225_Task_Speed_and_Accuracy_Decrease_When_Multitasking

Lippmann, L., Ryberg, R., Carney, R., & Moore, K. (2015). *Key "soft skills" that foster youth workforce success: Toward a consensus across fields*. Bethesda, MD: Child Trends. Retrieved from https://www.childtrends.org/wp-content/uploads/2015/06/2015-24AWFCSoftSkillsExecSum.pdf

Maharishi University of Management. (2014). Transcendental meditation reduces teacher stress and burnout, new research shows. Retrieved from https://www.eurekalert.org/pub_releases/2014-02/muom-tmr013014.php

Marsh, S. (2015). Five top reasons people become teachers—and why they quit. *The Guardian*. Retrieved from https://www.theguardian.com/teacher-network/2015/jan/27/five-top-reasons-teachers-join-and-quit

Marzano, R. J., Marzano, J. S., & Pickering. D. J. (2003). *Classroom management that works*. Alexandra, VA: ASCD.

Mulvahill, E. (2019). Five top reasons people become teachers—and why they quit. Retrieved from https://www.weareteachers.com/why-teachers-quit/

National Child Traumatic Stress Network. (n.d.). Secondary traumatic stress. Retrieved from https://www.nctsn.org/trauma-informed-care/secondary-traumatic-stress

National Council on Teacher Quality. (2014). Training our future teachers. Retrieved from https://www.nctq.org/dmsView/Future_Teachers_Classroom_Management_NCTQ_Report

National Life Group. (2017). *Lifechanger of the year nominee profile: Kelly Young.* Retrieved from http://app.lifechangeroftheyear.com/nomination_detail.cfm?NominationID =516&NominationYear=2017

Newport, C. (2016). *Deep work: Rules for focused success in a distracted world.* New York: Grand Central Publishing.

Pariser, S. (2018). *Real talk about classroom management.* Thousand Oaks, CA: Corwin.

Patel, S. (2013). *Cleaning snow off the wrong car* [Video file]. Retrieved from https:// www.youtube.com/watch?v=WJMBwBUP5CQ

Patricelli, V. (2016). Why can't nurses get a break? Retrieved from https://www .statnews.com/2016/09/23/nurses-break-patient-care/

Process Oriented Guided Inquiry Learning (POGIL). (2017). https://www.pogil.org

Pychyl, T. (2013). Strategies to strengthen executive function. Retrieved from https:// www.psychologytoday.com/us/blog/dont-delay/201302/strategies-strengthen -executive-function

Pychyl, T. (2018). ADHD and procrastination. Retrieved from https://www.psychology today.com/us/blog/dont-delay/201809/adhd-and-procrastination

Rabin, L. A., Fogel, J., & Nutter-Upham, K. E. (2011). Academic procrastination in college students: The role of self-reported executive functioning. *Journal of Clinical and Experimental Neuropsychology, 33*(3), 344–357

Sanfelippo, J. (2019). 4 steps to improving school culture. Retrieved from https://www .educationdive.com/news/4-steps-to-improving-school-culture/545901/

Secret teacher: Stress is reaching a crisis point in schools. (2013). *The Guardian.* Retrieved from https://www.theguardian.com/teacher-network/teacher-blog/2013/dec/28/ stress-crisis-teaching-profession-secret-teacher

Shavelson, R. (1981). Research on teachers' pedagogical thoughts, judgments, decisions, and behavior. *Review of Educational Research, 51*(4), 455–498.

Smith, E. (2014). *Using dialogue circles to support classroom management* [Video file]. Retrieved from https://www.youtube.com/watch?v=qTr4v0eYigM

Solomon, A. (2009). Notes on an exorcism. Retrieved from https://themoth.org/ stories/notes-on-an-exorcism

Sonorrari. (2017). 10 big companies that promote employee meditation. Retrieved from https://www.sonorrari.com/single-post/2017/04/06/10-Big-Companies-That -Promote-Employee-Meditation

Sparks, S. (2017). How teachers' stress affects students: A research roundup. Retrieved from https://www.edweek.org/tm/articles/2017/06/07/how-teachers-stress-affects -students-a-research.html

Steenbarger, B. (2017). Finding our greatness: Fresh perspectives on time management. *Forbes.* Retrieved from https://www.forbes.com/sites/brettsteenbarger/2017/10/20/ finding-our-greatness-fresh-perspectives-on-time-management/#79679bc01c42

Stice, J. (n.d.). Both educators and students are more stressed than ever, according to new studies. Retrieved from https://www.educationworld.com/a_news/both -educators-and-students-are-more-stressed-ever-according-new-studies-5488152

Taylor, S., Chowdhury, S., & Pychyl, T. (2018). Examining procrastination and delay among individuals with and without attention deficit hyperactivity disorder.

*World Academy of Science, Engineering and Technology, International Journal of Psychological and Behavioral Sciences 12*(7). Retrieved from https://waset.org/pdf/books/?id=95030&pageNumber=128

The Teaching Center. (2019). Using roles in group work. Retrieved from https://teaching center.wustl.edu/resources/active-learning/group-work-in-class/using-roles-in-group-work/

A teacher makes 1500 decisions a day. (2016). Retrieved from https://www.teachthought.com/pedagogy/teacher-makes-1500-decisions-a-day/

TeachThought. (2019). A teacher makes 1500 educational decisions a day. Retrieved from https://www.teachthought.com/pedagogy/teacher-makes-1500-decisions-a-day/

Terada, Y. (2018). Burnout isn't inevitable: Teachers are stressed—but schools can help. Retrieved from https://www.edutopia.org/article/burnout-isnt-inevitable

Tschabitscher, H. (2019). 19 fascinating email facts. Retrieved from https://www.lifewire.com/how-many-emails-are-sent-every-day-1171210

Tucker, C. (2013). The basics of blended instruction. Retrieved from http://www.ascd.org/publications/educational-leadership/mar13/vol70/num06/The-Basics-of-Blended-Instruction.aspx

Tucker, C. (2017). *Rethink your grading practices*. Retrieved from https://catlintucker.com/2017/12/grading-practices/

Wolpert-Gawron, H. (2009). Setting boundaries can mean a happier teaching career. Retrieved from https://www.edutopia.org/setting-boundaries-teachers

Wolpert-Gawron, H. (2019). Decluttering your classroom: Thoughtful reflection will help you make decisions about what to keep and what to discard in your classroom. Retrieved from https://www.edutopia.org/article/decluttering-your-classroom

Zee, M., & Koomen, H. M. Y. (2016).Teacher self-efficacy and its effects on classroom process, student academic adjustment, and teacher well-being: A synthesis of 40 years of research. *Review of Educational Research, 86*(4), 981–1015.

# Index

# Helping educators make the *greatest impact*

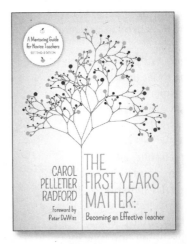

Corwin books represent the latest thinking from some of the most respected experts in K–12 education. We are proud of the breadth and depth of the books we have published and the authors we have partnered with in our mission to better serve educators and students.

## GRAVITY GOLDBERG

Can brilliant teaching boil down to five practices? Ahh—yes! This book applies ideas from fields of psychology, education, and science to name five key habits involving core beliefs, practice, relationships, professional growth, and one's whole self.

## VICTORIA LENTFER

The CALM method—Communication, Accountability, Leadership, and Motivation—provides an actionable framework for redirecting student behavior.

## ELAINE K. McEWAN-ADKINS

This teacher edition of a best-seller provides strategies to promote a healthy climate for communication to positively manage even the most difficult parent situations.

## MICHAEL McDOWELL

This book provides practices that strategically support students as they move from novices to experts in core academics.

A SAGE Publishing Company

## Helping educators make the greatest impact

**CORWIN HAS ONE MISSION:** to enhance education through intentional professional learning.

We build long-term relationships with our authors, educators, clients, and associations who partner with us to develop and continuously improve the best evidence-based practices that establish and support lifelong learning.